# MILK. MADE.

For Leonie, Tilla and Wilkie

# MILK. MADE.

## A BOOK ABOUT CHEESE

## HOW TO CHOOSE IT, SERVE IT AND EAT IT

NICK HADDOW

PHOTOGRAPHY BY ALAN BENSON

hardie grant books

# CONTENTS

INTRODUCTION .......................................... 10

# FROM THE DAIRY ............................ 14

## MILK ........................................................ 18
WHAT'S HAPPENED TO OUR DAIRY FARMS? ... 24
BREEDS OF DAIRY ANIMALS ............................ 38
INTERVIEW: TONGOLA DAIRY ........................ 46

## BUTTER .................................................. 50

## YOGHURT ............................................... 72
INTERVIEW: SUGAR HOUSE CREAMERY ......... 98

# CHEESE .................................................. 102

## FRESH CHEESES ................................. 112
WHEY CHEESE ................................................ 116
PDO AND PGI CHEESES ................................. 122
RAW MILK CHEESE ....................................... 132
NATURAL CHEESEMAKING ........................... 142
WHEY ............................................................ 144
INTERVIEW: LE SAPALET DAIRY ................... 150

# SURFACE-RIPENED CHEESES ... 154
WHAT'S THE DIFFERENCE BETWEEN
BRIE AND CAMEMBERT? ............................... 165
INTERVIEW: THE PINES DAIRY ..................... 176

# BLUE CHEESES .................................. 180
INTERVIEW: PARISH HILL CREAMERY ........... 200

# SEMI-HARD CHEESES ..................... 202
THE DARK ART OF MATURATION ................. 209
CHEESE AND WOOD ..................................... 218
INTERVIEW: WESTCOMBE DAIRY ................. 224

# COOKED CURD CHEESES ............. 228
INDUSTRIAL, ARTISANAL AND
FARMHOUSE CHEESES ................................. 246
INTERVIEW: FORT DES ROUSSES .................. 254
HIGH-ALTITUDE CHEESES ............................ 261

# SELECTING AND SERVING
CHEESE .................................................. 264

RESOURCES ............................................. 280

FURTHER READING ............................... 281

INDEX ...................................................... 284

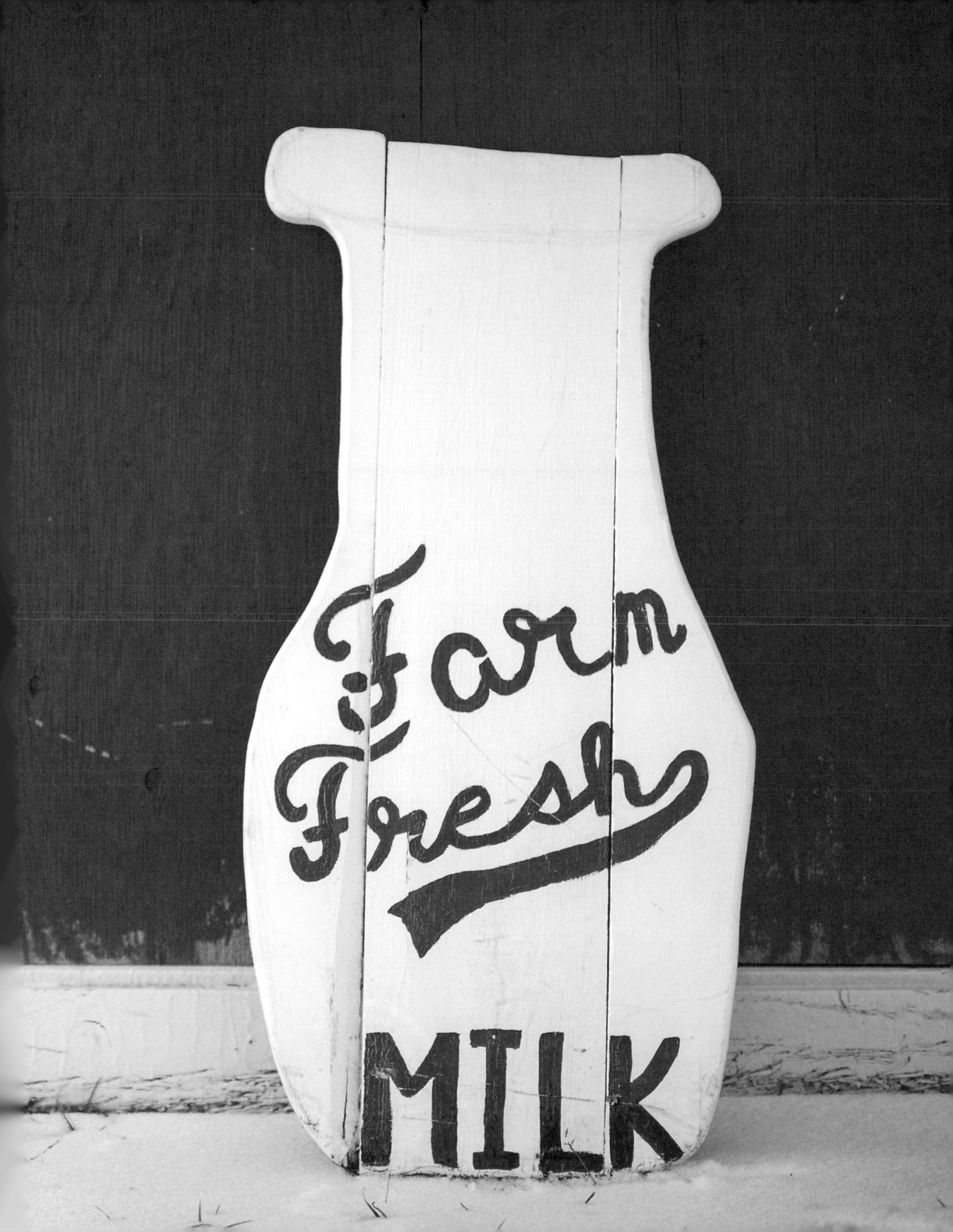
Farm
Fresh
MILK

# INTRODUCTION

## When I eat great cheese, I am taken somewhere else ...

To me, cheese is so much more than a food. In the oft-quoted words of Clifton Fadiman, 'it is milk's leap to immortality'. It is an expression of a craft which has been practised for millennia. It is the perfect manifestation of human agriculture – a word which itself sets us apart from all other animals on the planet: farming (agri) and society (culture). It illustrates our resourcefulness to provide food for ourselves and our families. And above all, it provokes one of our most fundamental human characteristics – our pursuit of pleasure, through the food we make and eat.

I often get asked why I got into cheese. I joke that it is primarily because I did not pay enough attention at school (there is some truth in that, I had a pretty privileged education and I am sure I am the only cheesemaker that the Collegiate School of St Peter has ever turned out). But really the answer is because I first got into food.

I grew up in Adelaide in the 70s and 80s. My home was a gentle and continual supply of tastes and smells. Mum was always a bit of a thrift – she was the child of Depression Era parents who valued the importance, as well as the economy, of a home where meals started with raw ingredients and real cooking. Growing up, one of my favourite things was following my mum around on our weekly trip to the Adelaide market where my senses would be assaulted by the piles of fruits and vegetables, the smell of fresh fish, roasting coffee and yeasty breads and the noisy shouts of Greek, Italian and Chinese immigrants hawking their produce. I was dazzled by the displays of produce, but especially the cheese counters. Fascinated by vast arrays of foreign names and intriguing forms, I wanted to know the history and stories behind each cheese.

My cheesy journey has taken me all around the world but it started in a kitchen in South Australia's Eden Valley. It was a small country restaurant, one that had an excellent reputation for using local produce. I had only been there a few days and it was my first job cooking commercially. A refrigerated van would pull up every week with our cheese order from Adelaide and being the low-ranking new kid, I got to unpack the deliveries. I opened the box from our cheesemonger and pulled out the buckets of cream, huge blocks of butter and the bags of grated parmesan. Then I pulled out two small rounds of a sheep's milk blue cheese from Meredith Dairy in Victoria. It was a revelation. The rind was grey and felt alive. The smell was incredible. It was earthy, like damp soil, and musty like a cellar. Inside, the cheese was ivory-coloured and the texture was somewhere between firm and soft. There were occasional pockets of blue-green mould. The flavour ... lanolin, salt, animal, earth, straw. I had no idea cheese could be like this. And so began my journey to understand what really makes great cheese great.

There have been many stops along the way. I have met with, made cheese with, milked with and talked late into the night with countless farmers, cheesemakers and affineurs in the pursuit of learning about real cheese around the world. I have made, aged and sold cheese everywhere from Ireland to India, but in 2003 I settled down on a small island off the south coast of Tasmania to start my own cheesemaking business.

My partner Leonie and I bought an old house on five acres on Bruny Island. We were broke, jobless and wanting to start our own cheese business on an island of only 600 people, with few tourists and no dairies, making a highly perishable product, marketed to people that lived hundreds or thousands of kilometres away. Bruny Island Cheese Co. was the most stupid, most naïve, most ambitious plan conceivable. And I would do it all again in a heartbeat.

For the first two years, we made cheese using plastic tubs we had bought at a $2 shop, some PVC pipe cut into short lengths and a few bakers' trays I had 'borrowed' from the back of a local supermarket. We transported the milk in 20 litre (5 gallon) buckets in the back of our VW Kombi, and we sold the cheese (illegally) from an antique display fridge in our lounge room. We worked from 6 am until 6 pm making cheese and then went and worked in a bar until midnight to make enough money to buy the milk to do it all again the following day.

Today, Bruny Island Cheese Co. is a bit more grown-up but it is still a pursuit of how to make great cheese, using traditional techniques, within the strict regulatory constraints of Australia. We push these boundaries as far as possible, firm in the belief that cheese can not only be made safely from raw milk but that it is vital for achieving regional character and to differentiate artisan cheesemakers from industrial producers.

Cheesemaking is often seen through the lens of either science or art, but rarely both. To me, it is neither. Cheesemaking is nature itself. In its most simple form, cheese is the fermentation and preservation of milk. This happens through a series of natural processes that have served us for thousands of years. Then science took over. In less than 100 years we have gained an incredible insight into the chemistry and microbiology of cheesemaking and we have used that knowledge to control the process and steer the outcome away from what may have resulted naturally.

Not 'held back' by the centuries of established practices and the geographical constraints of Old World cheesemakers, the young guns of New World countries like Australia, the US and New Zealand have used their scientific understanding of cheesemaking to innovate and develop new cheeses. These cheeses are of indisputably high quality but often lack the terroir or the true regional character, which comes after an age of making the same cheese, in the same way, in the same place. Often, the application of many traditional practices in a New World context is prevented by regulations that have been developed in the name of food safety. Combined with a growing trend of industrialised agriculture almost devoid of biodiversity, real cheese everywhere is under enormous pressure.

This book celebrates the best of both Old and New World cheesemaking. It is not a field guide to these cheeses. Instead, I want to take you on a journey that shows you the tradition of cheesemaking and how those traditions are being applied in new and different ways. This book will also help you close the gap between farm and cheese, giving you an appreciation of what quality farming looks like. I hope that it also helps you understand what is required to make a great cheese and how to spot one in the crowd. It will give you the information you need to make good choices about the cheese you buy, and having bought it, how to store it, serve it and cook with it.

11

Michel Béroud in his cellar at Rougemont, Switzerland.

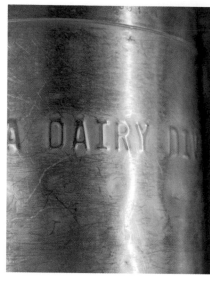
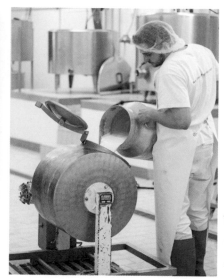

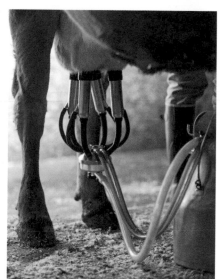

# FROM
# THE DAIRY

# Milk is bloody marvellous stuff! Just stop and think about what milk is for a moment …

Milk is the sum total of what an animal has eaten in the past few hours. Milk differs from animal to animal, from field to field and from farm to farm. From milk, we make the most incredible array of foods: butter, yoghurt, cheese and each of these comes in myriad forms, all of which are subtly influenced and informed by the specific geographical and biological conditions of the farm where that milk was made. This has a direct impact on the quality of the milk and the cheese, butter or yoghurt that is made from it.

Dairy cows are fed grass in a variety of forms including fresh grass, hay (dried grass), silage (fermented grass), grain (the seeds of grass varieties such as barley, oats of wheat) and maize (another form of grass). Goats and sheep prefer a wider diet that includes native herbs and perennials.

In Australia and New Zealand, many dairy farmers are in the enviable position to feed their animals on fresh, green grass 365 days of the year. In Europe and North America, animals are kept in sheds throughout the colder months and fed a diet of silage, hay and grain. Consequently, cheeses made in these regions have profound seasonal variation and are often sold as either 'winter' or 'summer' cheeses. (There is also a trend in industrial agriculture to house animals regardless of climatic need so that an animal's energy goes into milk production and is not 'wasted' on walking around a field.)

The factors that affect how, where and what grass grows include latitude, soil type, rainfall, soil microbes, temperature and indigenous insect populations. Whenever I visit a dairy farm, I habitually walk into the paddock and look at my feet and count the number of different plant species. Native pasture can literally have dozens of species of grasses, herbs and other plants. Native grasses provide a regional character to milk and cheese that introduced species cannot.

That's all great if you have abundant native grasses but in many countries where industrialised dairy farming takes place, we have replaced the natural biodiversity of native grasses with monoculture pastures such as clover, maize and lucerne (alfalfa). These often require greater inputs of fertiliser, water, herbicides and pesticides to be successful (which has a dramatic effect on soil microbes).

By comparison, native vegetation are well adapted to individual climates, provide drought relief, require less input and maintenance and are self-seeding. The problem with native pastures is that they are often less efficient in their regeneration, offer lower nutritional value and can carry less stock than exotic species.

As a cheesemaker, the quality of the milk and the specific characteristics on any given day fascinate me and guide how I treat that milk. This is a subtle business and it is only working with the same milk and making the same cheese for several years that I have begun to understand the complex relationship between the two.

My passion for milk in all its forms has taken me all around the world. I am constantly in search of products that reflect where they have been made by allowing the influences such as geography and breed to shine through the milk and then the cheese.

It disturbs me how bland and 'homogenised' dairy products have become around the world and how comfortable we are with this. Butter from Norway should be nothing like butter from New Zealand. Yoghurt made on the streets of India ought to be incomparable to yoghurt made in the Swiss mountains. And cheese … don't get me started!

If like me, good cheese makes you happy, then knowing a bit about where and how it was made is

essential to being able to make good choices as to what to buy. As the production of our food and farms becomes more globalised and industrialised, with it comes a loss of plant and animal diversity that results in a loss of food with regional character. In spite of this, farms that operate traditionally, sustainably and ethically are thriving around the world as people are seeking a stronger connection to their food and those who grow and make it. These are the farms where real butter, yoghurt and cheese comes from.

MILK

Good cheese cannot be made with bad milk. Bad cheese can be, and too often is, made with good milk. But, what really is milk? And what makes it either good or bad?

Let me state it as clearly as I possibly can: milk is the perfect food. It is safe and highly nutritious. Milk is the sole food source for every generation of new-born mammals and as such contains all that is needed for the baby to grow. Milk is the end result of a complex system that involves numerous moving parts and variables, each creating unique qualities in the final product.

Milk comes from ruminant animals that digest grass and convert the nutrients into protein using the mammary glands in their udders (in much the same way as humans do). For cows, which account for the vast majority of milk consumed on the planet, this involves several stages of digestion and it takes 50–70 hours to convert grass to milk. A cow needs to eat about 40 kg (90 lbs) of feed and drink about 50 litres (13 gallons) of water to produce about 20 litres (5 gallons) of milk a day.

Close your eyes and think about the origins of the carton of milk in your fridge ... Most of us conjure up an image of blue skies and green hills dotted with black and white cows happily grazing or lying in deep pasture, chewing their cud. Unfortunately, the majority of the world's dairy industry could not look more different. The vast majority of milk comes from cows of the same breed that are often housed in huge sheds, being fed a standardised and abnormal diet in order to produce unhealthy quantities of milk that has a reduced microflora of little or no regional character.

From a cheesemaking point of view, the best milk is unpasteurised and comes from healthy animals that are traditional to a region, which graze on multi-species or native pastures, drink clean water and are not forced to produce unnatural quantities of milk.

These animals will always produce high quality, safe milk with regional character and integrity, and will lead to cheese that has inherent quality and recognisable terroir.

## WHAT IS IN MILK?

Milk is basically a liquid in which a bunch of insoluble solids are floating around in suspension. Homogenisation is a modern process that emulsifies the natural cream in the milk, which means the cream doesn't rise to the top. A cheesemaker's job is to separate these solids from the liquid. In cheesemaking parlance, we call the liquid 'whey' and the solids 'curds'. These insoluble solids are mostly proteins and fats. Dissolved in the whey is lactose and a small amount of soluble protein.

The properties of milk from different animals differ hugely. And within each species, the variation in milk from different breeds can also be enormous.

### Fat

The different fats in milk are referred to as lipids. Fat exists in milk as small globules that vary in size and shape depending on the type and breed of the animal. The fat molecules in sheep's milk, for example, are tiny compared to cow's milk, making sheep's cheese more digestible. Because lipids are insoluble they are nearly all retained in the curd during the cheesemaking process.

If you have ever eaten low-fat cheese, you will appreciate just how important the fat in milk is to produce flavour, aroma and body. That said, there are plenty of great cheeses in the world where some or

all of the milk is skimmed. Cheddar and Parmigiano Reggiano are two classic examples and this probably comes from a time when the milk was skimmed of its valuable cream to produce butter alongside the cheese. Both these cheeses, however, are hard, low-moisture cheeses, so the fat content by weight is still comparatively high enough to contribute to flavour and aroma.

## Protein

Proteins form the bulk of milk solids and are vital in cheesemaking because they enable the milk to separate from the whey by binding together and forming a kind of matrix, locking in all the insoluble milk solids and allowing the whey to escape. There are two types of protein in milk – insoluble casein (about 78%) and whey protein which is soluble and, therefore, mostly lost when the whey is removed.

## Lactose

Lactose is the naturally occurring sugar in milk. Being a sugar it is soluble and therefore remains in the whey. Lactose is critical to cheesemaking, because it provides the food source for the bacteria which converts it to lactic acid (this is the fermentation step of cheesemaking). Milk is the only substance in which lactose is found and different dairy products contain different levels of lactose.

## Minerals

The most important minerals found in milk are calcium, phosphorous, potassium and magnesium. Apart from their important nutritional role, in cheesemaking they allow the whey to separate from the curds.

## Vitamins

Milk contains good quantities of vitamins A, E and B2 and small quantities of vitamins D, E, K, B1, B3 and B12. Some of these vitamins are very susceptible to heat treatment such as pasteurisation.

## Enzymes

In milk, many different enzymes arise naturally from bacteria in an animal's mammary glands and teat canals or from the micro-organisms that gain entry to the milk at a later stage, such as starter culture bacteria or the microflora that grows on cheese rinds. These enzymes have a profound effect on both the quality of the raw milk and the maturation of the cheese after manufacturing. Enzymes such as lipases, proteases and lactase hydrolyse (break down) the fats into different components. This process is vital in producing the delicate flavours and aromas found in good quality cheese. Unfortunately, pasteurisation removes many of these enzymes, thus greatly limiting the production of these complex flavours.

## MILK FROM DIFFERENT ANIMALS

Take a stroll down the dairy aisle of your local supermarket and you are likely to see cheese made from cow's, sheep's, goat's and even buffalo milk. But keep going to the milk section and the choice is usually just cow's milk (granted, it comes in a ridiculous and confusing number of varieties).

Around the world, however, milk sourced from camels, yaks, reindeer, elks, donkeys and horses is also consumed or made into cheese. The common thread to most of these animals is that they are all ruminants: a special type of mammal whose four-chambered stomachs allow the production of great amounts of milk from a high-fibre, low-nutrient diet. Of course, all mammals produce milk, but ruminants generally all have big teats, making them easy to milk.

We have been milking animals for approximately 12,000 years. Goats and sheep were probably domesticated first, followed by cows. Back then though, cows were called aurochs – a sort of grand wild ox that inhabited Europe, Asia and North Africa but became extinct in the 1600s. Aurochs were naturally fierce and stubborn animals, but after centuries of breeding they became the docile animal that we call cows today. Genetic diversity from breeding over hundreds of years created hundreds of different breeds in the same way that humans bred different kinds of dogs from their common predecessor, the wolf. These cows all had differing traits and over time, characteristics that were favourable to specific environments led to localised breeds and, subsequently, regional cheeses. Regrettably, the unique traits of these breeds and cheeses have become bastardised in recent history through globalisation, so that now the same cheeses are made from milk from the same breeds throughout the world.

Although cow's milk makes up over 80% of all milk consumed, milk from sheep, goats and buffalo produces some of the greatest and most iconic cheeses. From sheep we get powerhouse cheeses such as Roquefort, Manchego, Pecorino and Ossau-Iraty. Goat's milk gives us Crottin de Chavignon, Pouligny-Saint-Pierre, Valençay, Chabichou du Poitou and Garrotxa. And of course the ubiquitous Italian mozzarella comes from buffalo milk.

### Sheep's milk

Sheep's milk is high in fat and protein. This is a dream for cheesemakers because the milk is more responsive and yields much greater quantities of curd (it takes about 4 litres/4 quarts of sheep's milk to make 1 kg/2 lb 3 oz of cheese), but sheep provide far less milk than cows, 3–4 litres (3–4 quarts) per day at best, making them less efficient to farm as dairy animals. Another disadvantage is that sheep have a much shorter lactation cycle and are seasonal milkers.

Sheep's milk will commonly produce curd that is firm and robust, great for firmer cheeses and especially good for making thick, rich yoghurt and fresh cheese. The small size of the fat and protein particles means that sheep's cheese has a fine, silky texture. Containing no carotene, sheep's milk is almost pure white and sheep's cheese is generally ivory in colour. The high fat content means that poorly made sheep's cheese can have a slightly rancid flavour or lanolin character.

### Goat's milk

Goat's milk differs from cow's milk in that it is naturally homogenised, which means that the cream will not rise to the top to be separated.

Goats are also a bit pickier about what they eat and are browsers rather than grazers meaning they pick the tops off many different plant species and will even nibble on bark to get their nutrients. This varied diet produces complex and strong- flavoured cheeses. But goat's cheese should not have a strong, pungent 'buck' quality – this is the result of poor quality feed or the presence of hormone-inducing bucks in the herd.

A healthy goat will only produce up to 5 litres (5 quarts) of milk per day but that milk is beautifully delicate. Like sheep's milk it lacks carotene, resulting in milk and cheese that is porcelain white. The fat and protein molecules are also much smaller than those found in cow's milk, making it easier to digest and the preferred milk for people who struggle to eat cow's milk cheeses. Although the majority of goat's cheeses tend to be fresh, young cheeses that smack of delicious lactic acid, goat's milk can also be made into wonderful semi-hard and blue cheeses.

## Buffalo milk

Buffalo are native to the hot, humid climes of Asia where they have been domesticated for thousands of years and farmed for their hides, meat and milk. Still common in India, their milk is widely used to make curd, yoghurt, ghee and paneer and is an important part of the Indian vegetarian diet.

Buffalo came to Europe with Arab traders who first brought the animal to northern Africa and then to southern Italy, where it was perfectly suited to the hot climate and boggy plains around Naples. Buffalo are bovids, not bovines, which means the two cannot be cross-bred. They differ from bovine cows in that they lactate for longer (11 months) and their milk lacks carotene and is naturally homogenised. Buffalo milk also has a much higher percentage of milk solids than cow's milk, which is terrific for producing yoghurt and fresh cheeses such as the famed Mozzarella di Bufala from the Campania region behind Naples.

# HOW TO MAKE CRÈME FRAÎCHE

Crème fraîche is cream that has been allowed to mature under carefully controlled conditions so that the natural bacteria grows and converts lactose into lactic acid. This not only thickens the cream a little, but also gives it a wonderful light taste that makes it great to cook with. The more you let the cream ferment, the stronger the flavour will be and the thicker the result.

MAKES 500 G
(1 LB 2 OZ/2 CUPS)
500 ml (17 fl oz/2 cups)
   unthickened pure
   cream (36% fat)
2 tablespoons 'live' plain
   pot-set yoghurt

Combine the cream and yoghurt thoroughly in a medium-sized saucepan. Using a thermometer to assist you, warm the mixture to 25°C (77°F) then pour into sterilised glass jars. Seal each jar with a tightly fitting lid.

Place the jars in a small cooler or polystyrene box and pour in tepid tap water until it comes halfway up the sides of the jars. Set aside for 12–24 hours (you might need to change the water bath to keep it warm) until the cream appears thickened. (Don't shake the jars or the 'gel' will be destroyed.)

Once thickened, refrigerate the jars for up to 2 weeks. The crème fraîche will continue to thicken and develop in flavour even in the fridge.

## WHAT'S HAPPENED TO OUR DAIRY FARMS?

Around the world, modern dairy farms are the jewel in the crown of industrial agriculture, but sadly they are virtually unrecognisable from their counterparts even just a few decades ago. For example, of the 800 existing dairy breeds around the world, the vast majority of the 1.3 billion cows on the planet belong to a single breed. Like so many other areas of the agricultural landscape, the loss of biodiversity is huge.

Cows have become the unfortunate victims of the industrialisation of the dairy industry. One breed in particular, the ubiquitous black and white Holsteins (also known as Friesians), has suffered a hideous fate. Through decades of artificial and selective breeding practices, we have transformed this breed into one which is almost unrecognisable from its predecessors. Today, Holsteins are little more than milk factories on legs. Because of their incredible efficiency, they are the preferred breed in most milk-producing countries. They regularly produce up to 60 litres a day (compared to 12–15 litres a day for more traditional breeds) and consequently have increased stress placed on their bodies which restricts them to a shorter life span of 5–8 years, rather than the 15–20 year life a heritage breed cow might enjoy.

Where Holsteins are milked, you will usually also find dairy products that are lacking true character. By contrast, the examples of great cheese made from traditional breeds around the world are countless. For me, understanding the breed of animal behind the cheese is critical to understanding the quality and integrity of the cheese.

The economic landscape of dairy farming is also changing. In Australia, in 1985 there were 19,380 dairy farms and the average herd size was 93 cows. Today, there are only 6,128 dairy farms and the average herd size has tripled to 284 cows. Despite this huge reduction in farms our milk production has increased from 6 billion litres (1.6 billion gallons) to 10 billion litres (2.6 billion gallons).

More than three-quarters of the world's dairy cows are from a single breed, Holstein Friesians.

# PORK LOIN BRAISED IN MILK

I have eaten this dish in the north of Italy and in the south of Spain, so I have no idea where it comes from originally. This is a brilliant way to cook pork. The meat stays incredibly moist while the milk reduces to a thick, creamy sauce. It is really important to use good flavoured pork for this recipe, as there are not many ingredients to otherwise flavour the dish.

SERVES 6

100 g (3½ oz) butter
3 tablespoons extra-virgin olive oil
1 onion, finely chopped
4 garlic cloves, finely chopped
200 g (7 oz) pancetta, roughly chopped
1.2–1.5 kg (2 lb 10 oz– 3 lb 5 oz) boneless pork loin
1 litre (34 fl oz/4 cups) full-cream (whole) milk
250 ml (8½ fl oz/1 cup) thick (double/heavy) cream
4 fresh bay leaves
8 sage leaves, chopped, plus extra to garnish (optional)
zest of 1 lemon

Preheat the oven to 190°C (375°F).

Melt the butter in a heavy casserole dish with a lid (Dutch oven) over medium heat. Add the olive oil, onion, garlic and pancetta and cook, stirring, for 2–3 minutes, until the onion is golden and the pancetta is crisp. Remove from the heat and set aside in a bowl.

Rub the pork with salt and pepper all over and place in the casserole dish. Brown the outside of the pork loin over medium heat, turning every few minutes. Return the onion mixture to the pan and pour in the milk and cream. Add the bay leaves, sage and lemon zest.

Place the lid on the casserole dish and cook in the oven for 2½–3 hours, basting the pork with the sauce every 20–30 minutes, until the pork is very tender and the milk sauce has thickened. Transfer to a serving dish, cut into thick slices and serve with the milk sauce poured over the top. Garnish with a few extra sage leaves, if desired.

# NOT ROSS'S SAAG PANEER

There is an Indian restaurant not far from our place that makes a killer version of this classic dish. It was one of the best 'saags' I had ever tasted outside of India. That was, until my mate Ross O'Meara cooked his version for me. It was brilliant. He wouldn't give me the recipe, but then stupidly included it in our *Gourmet Farmer Deli Book*. So I copied it, fiddled with the spices and improved it. Nobody likes a show-off, mate!

It is very easy to make paneer, and it's a great way to use up excess milk. If you want to have a go at making your own, follow the recipe on page 116.

## SERVES 6

450 g (1 lb) fresh English spinach leaves or silverbeet (Swiss chard), white stalks removed and leaves chopped

50 g (1¾ oz) ghee or 45 ml (1½ fl oz) vegetable oil

300 g (10½ oz) paneer cheese, cut into bite-sized cubes

1 onion, finely chopped

3 garlic cloves, sliced

1 thumb-sized piece of fresh ginger, peeled and finely chopped

4 tomatoes, deseeded and chopped

½ teaspoon chilli powder

2 teaspoons curry powder

1 teaspoon ground coriander

1 teaspoon dried fenugreek leaves

¼ teaspoon turmeric

3 teaspoons garam masala

1 teaspoon salt

3 teaspoons lemon juice

unsalted butter, to serve

warm naan bread, to serve

cooked basmati rice, to serve

Boil the spinach or silverbeet in 600 ml (20½ fl oz) water for 5 minutes. Drain, reserving the cooking liquid. Mash or purée the greens and set aside.

Heat the ghee or oil in a frying pan with a lid over medium heat, and fry the cubes of paneer until lightly browned on all sides. Remove from the pan and set aside.

In the same pan over medium heat, fry the onion, garlic and ginger for 3–4 minutes. Add the tomato and sprinkle over the chilli and curry powders, ground coriander, fenugreek leaves and turmeric. Cook for a couple of minutes then add the garam masala and the salt. Cover and cook for a further 2–3 minutes.

Add the paneer, puréed spinach and lemon juice to the pan. If the mixture is dry, add up to 45 ml (1½ fl oz) of the spinach water to help moisten the curry.

Remove from the heat and serve with butter, warm naan bread and basmati rice.

# MILK PUDDINGS WITH
# ELDERFLOWER CARAMEL

This is the sort of little pudding that is perfect served alongside other desserts, such as apple crumble or pear tart. The milk is the star here so use really good, fresh unhomogenised milk if you can find it.

MAKES 6

3 eggs

1 egg yolk

340 ml (11½ fl oz/1⅓ cups) full-cream (whole) milk

70 ml (2¼ fl oz) thick (double/heavy) cream

80 g (2¾ oz/⅓ cup) caster (superfine) sugar

60 ml (2 fl oz/¼ cup) elderflower cordial

CARAMEL

50 g (1¾ oz) caster (superfine) sugar

2 tablespoons elderflower cordial

Preheat the oven to 145°C (285°F).

Place six small glass jars or serving glasses in the oven to warm for 10 minutes. Remove from the oven and set aside.

To make the caramel, place the sugar, 1 teaspoon water and the elderflower cordial in a small saucepan and stir over medium heat until the sugar dissolves and turns a light golden colour. Pour the caramel evenly among the glass jars and set aside.

Fill and boil the kettle.

To make the puddings, whisk the eggs and the egg yolk in a medium-sized stainless-steel bowl, until the mixture is a bit foamy. Set aside.

Place the milk, cream, sugar and elderflower cordial in a medium-sized saucepan over low heat and stir until combined and the mixture starts to steam. Do not let it boil. Remove from the heat and gradually add the egg mixture, stirring constantly. Carefully divide the mixture evenly among the jars.

Cover each jar with an aluminium foil 'lid' and stand in a deep baking dish. Fill the dish with boiling water until it reaches halfway up the sides of the jars. Cook in the oven for 25–35 minutes, until the puddings are set but still a little wobbly. Remove from the water bath and allow to cool slightly before serving.

These puddings can also be made the day ahead and are just as delicious served cold.

Margot Brooks and Alex Eaton at Sugar House
Creamery, in New York State, bottle raw milk for sale
from their herd of Brown Swiss cows. The milk is in
bottles within 30 minutes of the cow being milked.

# SPANISH FRIED MILK

You will find leche frita served throughout central and northern Spain. It is a sweet concoction of milk thickened with a touch of flour, fried in butter and dusted with sugar and spice. It is delicious served with coffee or poached fruit. The milky batter for this recipe is best made a day ahead to let it firm up.

SERVES 4

25 g (1 oz) cornflour (cornstarch)

55 g (2 oz) plain (all-purpose) flour

115 g (4 oz/½ cup) caster (superfine) sugar, plus extra for sprinkling

1 litre (34 fl oz/4 cups) full-cream (whole) milk

1 cinnamon stick

zest of 1 lemon

2 eggs

60 ml (2 fl oz/¼ cup) olive oil, for frying

2 tablespoons butter

1 teaspoon ground cinnamon

Combine the cornflour, half the flour and the sugar in a large heatproof bowl. Add 250 ml (8½ fl oz/1 cup) of the milk and mix well with a whisk. Leave to stand for 10 minutes.

Heat the remaining milk with the cinnamon stick and lemon zest in a large saucepan over low–medium heat. When the milk begins to froth up, remove the cinnamon stick and pour the milk gradually over the sugar and flour mixture, whisking constantly until you have a smooth batter.

Pour the batter back into the pan and stir constantly over low heat for 10 minutes, until thickened.

Lightly oil a 20 cm (8 in) square baking dish. Pour in the batter – it needs to be at least 2 cm (¾ in) deep, or it will be difficult to manage later when frying. Place in the fridge to chill for a minimum of 3 hours, but overnight is better.

Turn out the batter onto silicone paper and cut into 5 cm (2 in) squares.

Beat the eggs in a medium-sized bowl. In a small deep frying pan, heat the olive oil and butter over medium heat. (The oil and butter should come up the side of the frying pan by at least 1 cm/½ in.)

Lightly coat each square with the remaining flour and dip quickly into the beaten egg before placing carefully in the hot oil and butter. Fry each side for about 1 minute or until golden brown. Drain briefly on paper towel before sprinkling with the extra sugar and dusting with cinnamon. Serve hot.

34

# SOUTH AMERICAN BUTTERMILK DOUGHNUTS FILLED WITH DULCE DE LECHE

Dulce de leche is just about the best thing you can do to milk, after making cheese, of course. It is the wondrously delicious result of milk and sugar that has been slowly simmered for hours, until the sugar caramelises and the milk evaporates leaving a rich, golden sweet syrup. Use it to layer cakes, dollop on scones or ice cream or to make these moreish buttermilk doughnuts. Lots of recipes call for sweetened condensed milk when making dulce de leche, but that's cheating and will give you a grainy texture. The real thing, using milk, is a bit more work but the result is far better.

## MAKES 18 SMALL DOUGHNUTS

### DULCE DE LECHE
MAKES 350–525 G (12½ OZ–
1 LB 3 OZ/1 – 1½ CUPS)
1 litre (34 fl oz/4 cups) milk
285 g (10 oz/1¼ cups) sugar
¼ teaspoon bicarbonate of
  soda (baking soda)
1 vanilla bean, split and
  seeds scraped

### DOUGHNUTS
1 tablespoon active dry yeast
2 tablespoons warm water
485 g (1 lb 1 oz/3¼ cups)
  plain (all-purpose) flour,
  plus extra for dusting
3 tablespoons light brown
  sugar
1 teaspoon salt
4 tablespoons butter, melted
  and cooled
3 egg yolks
1 vanilla bean, split and
  seeds scraped
1½ teaspoons ground
  cinnamon
250 ml (8½ fl oz/1 cup)
  buttermilk
115 g (4 oz/½ cup) caster
  (superfine) sugar
1 cup dulce de leche
vegetable oil for frying

To make the dulce de leche, stir together the milk, sugar, bicarbonate of soda and vanilla bean and seeds in a medium-sized heavy-based stockpot over medium heat. Bring to the boil, then reduce the heat and simmer uncovered, stirring frequently, until the mixture has caramelised and thickened. This will take at least a couple of hours and is best done slowly rather than rushing it – you want to end up with a deliciously thick, golden brown caramel liquid. Be careful towards the end of the cooking time that the mixture does not catch on the bottom of the pot and burn. Remove from the heat and discard the vanilla bean. Transfer the dulce de leche to a sterilised glass jar and seal while it is still hot. Leave to cool completely before placing in the fridge, where it will keep for up to 4 weeks.

To make the doughnuts, dissolve the yeast in the warm water in a small bowl and set aside (it should start to look foamy after a few minutes).

Combine 450 g (1 lb/3 cups) of the flour, the brown sugar and salt in the large bowl of an electric mixer fitted with a dough hook attachment. Add the butter, egg yolks, yeast mixture, vanilla bean seeds, ½ teaspoon of the ground cinnamon and buttermilk and knead until the mixture is smooth and silky. Alternatively, you can use your hands if you don't have an electric mixer. Add a little of the remaining flour if you need to stiffen up the dough a bit (it should resemble bread dough).

Place the dough in a large lightly oiled bowl. Cover with plastic wrap and set aside in a warm place to prove for 2–4 hours or until the dough has doubled in size. Knock back the dough and place in the fridge to chill and stiffen.

On a lightly floured work surface, roll the dough out until it is 2 cm (¾ in) thick. Cut the dough into rounds using a 4 cm (1¼ in) biscuit (cookie) cutter. Reroll any leftover dough until it is all used – you should have about 18 rounds. Place on a baking tray dusted with flour and cover with plastic wrap.

Set aside to rise in a warm place until they have doubled in size. Meanwhile, combine the sugar and remaining cinnamon in a medium-sized bowl and set aside. Spoon the dulce de leche into a piping bag fitted with a ½ cm (¼ in) plain piping nozzle.

Heat the oil in a wok or heavy-based saucepan to 190°C (375°F) or until a cube of bread dropped into the oil turns brown in 15 seconds. Fry 3–4 doughnuts at a time, turning them carefully with a fork until they are golden brown all over. Remove from the oil and drain on a plate with paper towel.

While they are still warm, pipe a small amount of dulce de leche into each doughnut, then roll in the sugar mixture to cover the outside of the doughnuts. Serve immediately.

# BREEDS OF DAIRY ANIMALS

## BREEDS OF COW

### Holstein Friesian
Originating from the Netherlands, these cattle are by far the most common breed, worldwide. Extremely efficient, resilient and versatile, Holsteins are the result of rigorous breeding over the past 150 years. They are highly regarded for their ability to produce large quantities of milk, but it is often lacking in character.

### Jersey
The femme-fatale of breeds. Named after the English Channel Island from which they originate, Jersey cattle earned their reputation for producing rich milk, high in butterfat in the 1900s, when they were the preferred breed for producing butter.

### Brown Swiss
This breed is famed for producing milk of good quality and quantity and is traditionally used to make mountain cheeses such as Sbrinz. It is also used, albeit rarely, as a commercial breed in the US, UK, Australia and New Zealand.

### Australian Dairy Shorthorn
Shorthorn cattle can be traced back to the 16th century in Great Britain; they are the oldest recorded breed existing in the world today and one that has played a vital role in the Australian dairy industry.

Dairy Shorthorns are big, strong-framed cattle with hardy constitutions, and they produce excellent quality milk in good quantities.

### Ayrshire
A tough-as-boots Scottish breed that resulted from cross-breeding local cows with cows native to the Channel Islands. Ayrshires were at one time the preferred breed throughout the UK, but are now rarely seen.

### Simmental
A true dual-purpose breed, which is rarely used for milking outside its native home of Switzerland. It is the traditional breed for Emmentaler.

### Tarentaise
An important breed in the French Alps where it remained isolated and with pure blood-lines until relatively recently. This breed is now being milked commercially in the US and Canada.

### Dexter
A small Irish breed that has clawed its way back from the brink of extinction. Popular with small holders because of its size, Dexters are low-producing but their milk is of a similar quality to Jerseys.

## BREEDS OF SHEEP

### East Friesian
This breed originates from Germany and, like its bovine namesake, has a reputation for producing large quantities of milk. Globally, it is often the preferred breed due to a long lactation period, but their fragile constitution means they are often cross-bred with local, hardier breeds.

### Manchega
The famous Spanish cheese Manchego is made exclusively from the milk of this breed. This tough sheep inhabits the hot, central plains of the La Mancha region in Spain.

### Lacaune
After East Friesian, this is possibly the most popular dairy sheep. Hardy, good milkers, this breed originates from the Massif-Central region of France where its milk is used to make the famous Roquefort cheese.

### Comisana
Probably the most important dairy sheep breed in Italy, Comisana are indigenous to Sicily and are used to make pecorino cheese.

A Brown Swiss tethered to be milked at
Sugar House Creamery in New York State.

An East Friesian ewe and lamb at Pecora Dairy, in Robertson, New South Wales.

### Awassi

A Middle Eastern dual-purpose breed that is famous for having fat tails used for storing energy to survive the tough conditions of the desert. For this reason, they are highly regarded in parts of Australia and the US where they are sometimes cross-bred with East Friesians or other breeds to boost their milking quality.

### Manech

This breed is used exclusively to make Ossau-Iraty in the Basque region of France. Manech come in red-headed and black-headed forms and graze the plains and mountains respectively.

## BREEDS OF GOAT

### Saanen

This breed originates from Switzerland. With their white coats, Saanens are very attractive animals. They are also the most abundant dairy goats across Australia, USA and Europe. They are highly productive but their milk is relatively low in milk solids.

### Toggenburg

Like Saanens, this is another Swiss breed. 'Toggies' range from fawn to brown and are a cool-climate mountain breed. They are good milkers, producing milk with an average butterfat content.

### Alpine

Swiss or French Alpines come in a variety of colours and are very hardy and adaptable animals, farmed in a huge variety of conditions. They are exceptionally good milkers but can tend to produce milk with low milk solids.

British Alpines are black with white markings. They originate from cross-breeding Toggenburgs, native British goats and Nubian goats in the early 1900s.

### La Poitevine

Think goat's cheese and you think of France, and this breed is the original breed of the Poitou-Charentes region where some of the world's best goat's cheese is made. Tragically, this breed is now considered endangered, having been replaced with much higher-yielding breeds.

### Anglo-Nubian

Despite their long floppy ears and faces that only their mothers could love, this breed is often placed on a pedestal. Cross-bred from local and exotic breeds from India and North Africa in Britain in the 1890s, they produce medium quantities of milk of excellent quality.

Saanen doe at Sleight Farm, Timsbury, in the UK.

Sheep gather on a patch of sunbathed grass not yet covered by oncoming winter snow at Vermont Shepherd, Vermont, USA.

# CHERRY CLAFOUTIS

A clafoutis is one of the easiest desserts you can make. It is basically a sweet custard, with enough of a backbone that you can load it up with fruit without it collapsing under pressure. You can pit the cherries if you like, but I'm too lazy – they provide a nice almond flavour – just remember you've left them in when eating!

**SERVES 6**

500 g (1 lb 2 oz) fresh sweet
    cherries
75 g (2¾ oz) caster
    (superfine) sugar
3 tablespoons kirsch
20 g (¾ oz) butter, melted,
    plus extra to grease
2 tablespoons light brown
    sugar
50 g (1¾ oz/⅓ cup) plain
    (all-purpose) flour
zest of 1 lemon
pinch of salt
2 eggs, beaten
270 ml (9 fl oz) full-cream
    (whole) milk
icing (confectioners') sugar,
    to dust

Place the cherries in a medium-sized bowl and lightly crush the fruit with the end of a rolling pin or glass bottle so that their skins break but not so they are pulverised. Stir through the caster sugar and kirsch. Cover with plastic wrap and set aside for a couple of hours.

Preheat the oven to 170°C (340°F).

Using the extra butter, lightly grease a baking dish big enough to fit the cherries in a single layer. Sprinkle over half of the light brown sugar.

Combine the flour, the remaining sugar, lemon zest and salt in a large bowl. In a separate bowl, whisk together the beaten egg, milk and melted butter, then gradually whisk this mixture into the flour mixture until you have a smooth batter that is free of lumps. Stir in the cherries and their juice, then pour the lot into the prepared baking dish.

Bake for about 30 minutes or until the clafoutis is set, but still pretty wobbly and golden brown on top. Allow to cool for about 15 minutes before dusting with icing sugar. Serve immediately.

42

# LEMON CRÈME FRAÎCHE ICE CREAM

When I was growing up, a special treat was to be taken to a shop called Flash Gelato. Their lemon gelati was so intensely sour, it felt like your underpants were in danger of disappearing. As I have matured, I still love that same lemony tang, but this ice cream, adapted from a Greg Malouf recipe, presents it in a rich, creamy form, perfect for accompanying most cakes and tarts.

MAKES JUST OVER 1 LITRE
(34 FL OZ/4 CUPS)
2 lemons
300 ml (10 fl oz) full-cream
    (whole) milk
170 g (6 oz/¾ cup) caster
    (superfine) sugar
50 g (1¾ oz) glucose syrup
1 vanilla bean, split and
    seeds scraped
7 egg yolks
550 g (1 lb 3 oz) crème fraîche

Remove the peel from the lemons with a vegetable peeler, being careful to get as little of the white pith as possible. Set aside. Slice the lemon in half and squeeze the juice into a cup through a tea strainer to remove any seeds or pulp. Set the juice aside.

Combine the milk, sugar, glucose, vanilla bean and seeds and lemon peel in a medium-sized saucepan, and stir over low heat until the sugars are dissolved. Remove from the heat and set aside.

Whisk the egg yolks in a large bowl. Continue to whisk and very slowly pour the hot milk liquid in a steady stream until completely combined. Place the mixture in a large saucepan and cook over a low heat, stirring constantly, for about 10 minutes or until the custard noticeably thickens and coats the back of a spoon. Remove from the heat and strain into a bowl to remove the lemon peel and vanilla bean.

Immediately place the custard in the fridge to chill – it will cool down more quickly if you stir it occasionally. Once the custard is completely cold, whisk in the crème fraîche and the lemon juice. Place in an ice-cream machine and churn according to the manufacturer's instructions. Remove from the churn and transfer to plastic containers. Freeze for at least 2 hours before serving.

This ice cream will keep in the freezer for up to 1 month.

44

# TONGOLA DAIRY

Hans and Ester are the real deal. Originally from Switzerland, they emigrated to southern Tasmania in 2003, where they carved out a small farm in the hills behind the town of Cygnet.

Hans Stutz and Ester Haeusermann are both highly creative as well as being deep thinkers. Every aspect of their farm and cheese production is subject to deep consideration with sustainability and ethical conduct being important touchstones.

Their farm was nothing more than a hillside covered with stringy-bark eucalyptus trees when they began. They designed and built every building themselves, using materials from their property or those they found locally and repurposed.

Hans and Ester have a small herd of Toggenburg goats that graze the native pastures and eucalypt woods. Their cheesemaking is just about as low-tech as you can go in Australia, which helps to preserve the quality of the milk. They make mainly lactic fresh cheeses and an interesting semi-hard washed-rind cheese called Billy.

This is the sort of operation that defies the strict regulatory framework imposed on cheesemakers in Australia. Tongola Dairy is an anathema because it's tiny and the farm is completely run by the owners with a very hands-on approach. If there are problems with a goat or a batch of cheese, Hans and Ester will know immediately.

Tongola Dairy, and those farms and cheesemakers like it, should be celebrated and supported because they are not only producing great cheese, they are creating truly regional cheese in a world where this is becoming harder to do and even harder to find.

**WHY DID YOU LEAVE A COUNTRY LIKE SWITZERLAND THAT HAS CENTURIES OF CHEESEMAKING HERITAGE, PEDIGREE AND TRADITION TO COME TO TASMANIA TO MAKE CHEESE?**

*There are two reasons. Firstly, it would be much harder to do what we do in Switzerland. Land is very expensive and there are lots of cheesemakers, which means lots of competition. Secondly, we love Australia and are much happier here!*

46

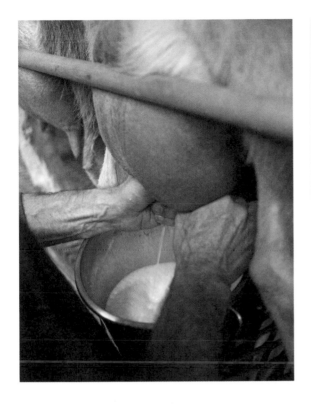

**DOES THE CHEESEMAKER IN YOU NOT WANT TO SWAP THE REGULATIONS AND THE UNDEVELOPED MARKETS OF AUSTRALIA FOR THE TRADITION AND RICH CHEESE CULTURE OF SWITZERLAND?**

*Not really. We like to bring our traditions to Australia. Making cheese here has more freedom – we can develop new cheeses here and have a free hand to do what we want. In that way we like not being bound by tradition.*

**WHEREVER I GO IN THE WORLD, DAIRY GOAT FARMERS ALL SEEM TO HAVE A UNIQUE BOND WITH THEIR ANIMALS – WAY MORE THAN SHEEP OR COW FARMERS. WHAT IS IT ABOUT GOATS THAT MAKES THEM SO SPECIAL?**

*Goats have individual personalities. Working with them on a daily basis really proves this. They each have their own characteristics. This makes goats harder to farm, because you have to treat them all as individuals, not as a herd, but it also makes farming them much more interesting.*

**WHEN YOU STARTED THE FARM AND CHEESERY, HOW DID YOU DECIDE WHAT CHEESES TO MAKE?**

*We tried to bring new flavours and aromas to Australia to help people appreciate that there is more to cheese than just cheddar! But also the market will influence what you make because you need to keep selling cheese to stay in business. We are still a bit disappointed that our Billy cheese is not more appreciated – most people just want to buy our fresh-curd cheese.*

**YOU BOTH WORK CLOSELY TOGETHER AND HAVE A SUCCESSFUL BUSINESS AND A SUCCESSFUL RELATIONSHIP. HAS THAT BEEN EASY TO ACHIEVE?**

*A personal relationship is no different from a working relationship. Both require tolerance and the willingness to compromise. It's just how life is. But, both our relationship and our business started small and grew bigger, so we have had plenty of time to learn how to get it right!*

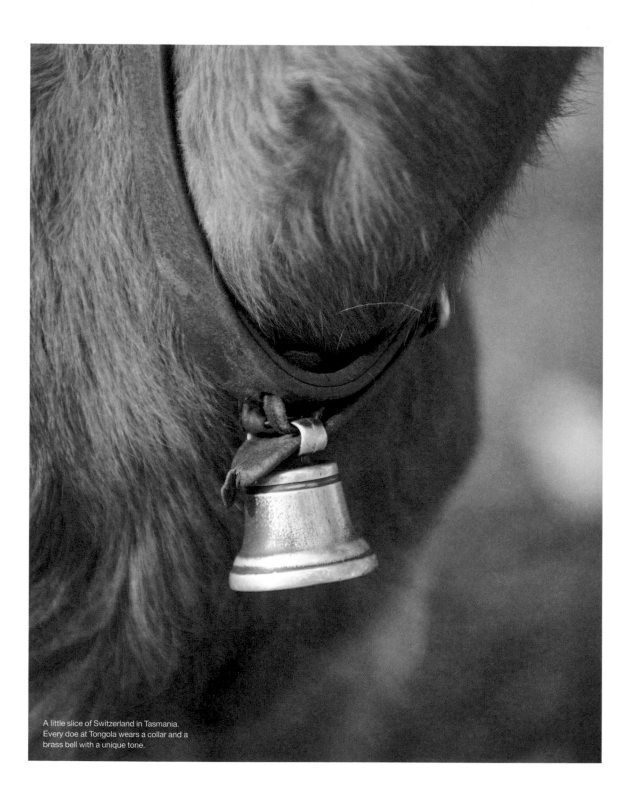

48

A little slice of Switzerland in Tasmania.
Every doe at Tongola wears a collar and a
brass bell with a unique tone.

# BUTTER

Ok, so it's not a cheese, but butter is a vital and traditional part of the whole dairy story. And, there are few things better than beautiful butter. Unfortunately, like cheese, a lot of butter made commercially today is rubbish.

Butter is made from the cream in milk and it's basically the separation of the butterfat from the buttermilk. This is done through agitation, or churning, where the membrane of the butterfat molecule is damaged and allows the fat particles to join together and separate from the liquid part of the cream, which is called the buttermilk. The buttermilk is drained off and the small grains of butter are usually rinsed and worked together to form butter through a process similar to kneading. Traditionally, this was done using wooden scotch hands (or butter beaters) to remove as much of the buttermilk as possible from the butter.

Hand-made butter will retain as much as 30% moisture, whereas butter made using modern techniques can have as little as half that amount. Consequently, this gives the butter a longer shelf life without requiring the addition of salt as a preservative.

Commercial butter is 80–82% milk fat, 16–17% water, and 1–2% milk solids (other than fat). It may also contain salt, added directly to the butter in concentrations of 1–2%. In the USA and Australia, butter must contain 80% minimum butterfat by law, while in France, butter must be composed of at least 82% fat. Home-churned butter on the other hand, can contain as much as 86% butterfat.

The vast majority of butter is made from cow's milk because of its natural ability to separate, allowing the cream that rises to the top to be carefully skimmed off. Sheep's and goat's milk is naturally homogenised, meaning their smaller fat molecules stay in suspension in the milk, making them harder to separate.

Historically, butter was made everywhere animals were milked, but what we recognise as butter today is most akin to butter from the cold, Scandinavian parts of Europe where it was stored for months in barrels or buried in peat bogs, developing a strong, peaty flavour as it aged. This practice was brought to Britain and Ireland by the Vikings, and even today, great butter is still associated with Scandinavia, along with butter from France, Belgium and Spain. Butter from these regions is geographically protected.

Mass-produced butter is rarely fermented because it is an additional, time-consuming step that is all about flavour and quality. It therefore has very little character and is manufactured to be stored for very long periods, often frozen. Consequently, mass-produced butter can often be rancid, which occurs through oxidation. When selecting butter, choose one that is made in small batches from cream that has been traditionally fermented. Alternatively, try making your own (see page 54).

### Cultured butter
Traditionally, all butter was cultured as a result of the cream being taken over several days' milking and the lack of refrigeration that would slow down the natural culturing processs. The lactose in the raw cream (which is full of naturally occurring bacteria) would begin to ferment, producing lactic acid. This increase in acidity would not only give the butter a pleasant sour taste but would also improve its keeping qualities.

Modern, mass-produced cultured butter is instead 'cultured' by adding lactic acid directly to the butter, or through the addition of bacteria, which rely on the

separating the remaining butterfat from the whey after cheese has been made. Whey is fermented as part of the cheesemaking process, which gives this butter a delicious, strong flavour. The problem is that butterfat in whey is found in such tiny quantities that the yield is very low and rarely seen to be worth the effort. But in places where they make a lot of cheese and generate a lot of whey and also have a no-waste mentality, this is where you will find excellent whey butter.

Look for whey butter from the Parma region (where they make Parmigiano Reggiano), the Fontina area of Aosta in Italy and from southwest England where cheddar is produced.

### Ghee

Ghee is used widely throughout India and South-East Asia. It is butter that has had most of its water and milk solids removed, leaving just the pure butterfat. This is achieved by slowly melting the butter and allowing it to separate – the whey protein comes to the top and can be skimmed off while the milk protein (casein) will sink. Ghee differs from clarified butter in that it is simmered to the point where the milk solids caramelise, giving the ghee a nutty flavour. Clarified butter is separated as soon as the butter has reached melting point and the water has evaporated.

### Buttermilk

The best buttermilk is a luscious liquid that is the byproduct of making cultured butter. It is sweet but also slightly acidic from the fermentation of the cream and it leaves the mouth feeling clean. By contrast, the buttermilk most commonly sold in supermarkets is usually made from reconstituted skimmed milk powder to which lactic acid is added. Ironically, it is often made by the large corporations that also make butter but throw away the real buttermilk because it does not have the shelf-life of the manufactured stuff. Go figure! Buttermilk is low in fat because almost all of the fat has gone into the butter. It is terrific to bake with and also to marinate meat because the lactic acid helps to tenderise the proteins.

long storage of the butter to develop acidity. Salt was traditionally added to help preservation, but these days, with refrigeration, it is mainly added for flavour.

Look for butter made in small batches on farms or by artisans. This butter is more likely to be properly cultured to achieve a better flavour.

### Sweet butter

Sweet (or uncultured) butter is a comparatively modern product that was born with the introduction of cream separators and refrigeration. Uncultured butter can be salted or unsalted and is generally inferior in flavour and aroma to cultured butter. There is no bacterial fermentation to contribute complexity, so the flavour is derived solely from the cream. Sweet butter is sometimes preferred by bakers or patisseries for its more neutral flavour.

### Whey butter

Not very common, but absolutely worth trying if you ever come across it, whey butter is made by

# HOW TO MAKE CULTURED BUTTER

If you can whip cream, you can make butter. Making cultured butter is not hard and the results will make the commercial stuff look like a block of grease in comparison.

MAKES 1 KG (2 LB 3 OZ)
1.5 litres (51 fl oz/6 cups)
   pure cream (35% fat),
   without thickeners
2 tablespoons 'live' yoghurt
   or cultured buttermilk (this
   will provide the bacteria to
   ferment the cream)
500 ml (17 fl oz/2 cups)
   chilled water
1 tablespoon sea salt
   (if making salted butter)

Make sure that all of your equipment is sterilised before using, to avoid cross-contamination.

Pour the cream into a large glass jar and stir in the yoghurt until well combined. Seal the jar with plastic wrap or a lid and leave to stand at room temperature (about 20°C/68°F) for 12–24 hours. This will initiate the fermentation process and develop the lactic acid. The longer you leave the mixture, the stronger the flavour of the butter will be. Chill the cream in the fridge for 2 hours before churning, as this allows the butter granules to form more easily.

Transfer the cream to either a domestic butter churn or an electric mixer with a whisk attachment and start to churn. As the cream turns to butter it will go through a few stages: first it will become whipped cream, then small grains of butter will appear; this is closely followed by the separation of the buttermilk and the butter granules becoming larger. At this stage, the buttermilk will need to be poured off to stop it from splashing out of the mixing bowl. Retain the buttermilk for cooking or for use as a culturing agent to make more butter or fresh cheese. It will keep in a sterilised glass jar in the fridge for up to 5 days.

Keep churning until the butter granules come together (this should only take a few mintues). At this point, pour off any remaining buttermilk and add the chilled water to the butter while you churn some more (this helps to wash the remaining buttermilk out of the butter). Drain the water and discard.

Tip the washed butter onto a clean wooden board. If you are making salted butter, sprinkle over the salt. Using clean wet hands (or wooden butter beaters if you have them), gently work the butter together, kneading and squeezing out as much moisture as possible for about 5 minutes.

Shape the butter into four blocks, wrap tightly in greaseproof paper or foil and place in an airtight container. The butter will keep in the fridge for up to 3 weeks, but it can also be wrapped tightly in plastic wrap and stored in the freezer. Frozen, unsalted butter will keep for 5–6 months and salted butter will keep for 9 months.

Forming sheep's milk butter at Le Sapalet, Switzerland. Note the pale ivory colour.

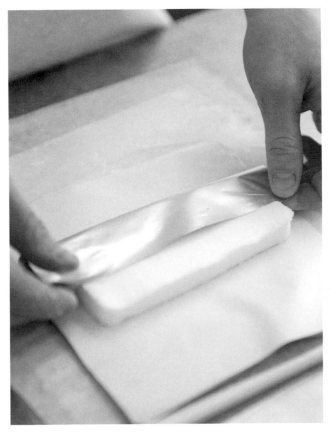

# CAFÉ DE PARIS BUTTER

This is a classic recipe that makes steak sing. If you are not a meat eater then don't despair, it also does wonders for steamed spuds or asparagus. There are 1001 versions of this but I have it on good authority that this is the original recipe created by Chef Dumont at the Café de Paris in Geneva in 1941. You can fiddle with it if you like to make your own version.

MAKES 12–14 SERVES
600 g (1 lb 5 oz) unsalted butter, softened
30 g (1 oz) tomato sauce (ketchup)
3 teaspoons Dijon mustard
15 g (½ oz) capers, rinsed and finely chopped
60 g (2 oz) finely diced shallots
1 tablespoon finely chopped flat-leaf parsley
1 tablespoon snipped chives
1 teaspoon dried marjoram
1 teaspoon finely chopped dill
1 teaspoon finely chopped thyme leaves
1 teaspoon finely chopped tarragon leaves
½ teaspoon finely chopped rosemary leaves
1 garlic clove, finely chopped
8 anchovy fillets, rinsed and finely chopped
1 tablespoon brandy
1 tablespoon madeira
1 teaspoon Worcestershire sauce
½ teaspoon paprika
½ teaspoon curry powder
¼ teaspoon cayenne pepper
juice of 1 lemon
zest of ½ lemon
zest of ¼ orange
2 teaspoons sea salt

In a large bowl, beat the butter by hand or use an electric mixer set to slow speed, until it has a slightly creamy texture.

In a separate bowl, combine all the other ingredients and mix thoroughly. Add this mixture to the butter and beat again until all the ingredients are completely combined.

Place a double thickness of foil, about 30 cm (12 in) long, on a flat surface and line with a similar-sized piece of silicone paper. Spread half the butter along one of the foil edges and roll up to form a long sausage shape – roll it with you hands like a rolling pin to get a tidy shape and eliminate any air pockets. Twist the ends to seal. Repeat this process with the remaining butter. Place in the fridge to chill before use.

To use, slice a 1 cm (½ in) thick disc of butter and place on top of a grilled steak (or a steamed spud). Traditionally, the steak is placed back under a hot grill (broiler) to soften and brown the butter, but I don't reckon you need to do this, just let it melt from the heat of the steak.

The butter can be stored in an airtight container in the fridge for a few weeks or in the freezer for several months.

57

# SIMPLE LEMON BUTTER SAUCE FOR SEAFOOD

Living on an island, I have grown to be pretty fussy about the seafood I eat. I rarely eat fish or shellfish that I have not caught myself and, when I cook fish, it is usually very simply pan-fried or barbecued. To me, the only thing that can make fresh fish taste better is a simple lemon butter sauce. Use this for anything from poached salmon to grilled crayfish.

MAKES ABOUT 125 ML
(4 FL OZ/½ CUP)
250 g (9 oz) unsalted
   cultured butter
2 garlic cloves, very finely
   chopped
1 tablespoon plain (all-
   purpose) flour
3 tablespoons lemon juice
1 teaspoon freshly ground
   black pepper
2 teaspoons finely chopped
   flat-leaf parsley

Melt half of the butter in a saucepan over medium heat. Add the garlic and cook, stirring, for about 2–3 minutes (do not let the mixture go brown or it will taste bitter).

Add the remaining butter and the flour and reduce the heat to low. Stir with a whisk to melt the butter and combine the flour, then stir in the lemon juice, pepper and parsley. Cook for a couple of minutes to thicken the sauce.

Remove from the heat and set aside for a few minutes. Whisk just before serving to emulsify the sauce.

58

# BUTTERMILK FRIED CHICKEN

There are few things more satisfying than good fried chicken. There are two secrets: the first is to brine the chicken as this ensures that the meat is moist and juicy and seasoned from the inside; the second is buttermilk, which makes the spicy coating on the chicken super crispy. You can make this dish a couple of hours ahead and keep it warm in the oven (just don't cover it or it will lose its crispness).

SERVES 6

6 chicken drumsticks
6 chicken thighs
6 chicken wings, wing tips removed
300 g (10½ oz/2 cups) plain (all-purpose) flour
75 g (2¾ oz/½ cup fine polenta (cornmeal)
60 g (2 oz/½ cup) cornflour (cornstarch)
2 teaspoons freshly ground black pepper
2 teaspoons paprika
1 teaspoon smoked paprika
1 teaspoon onion powder
1 teaspoon garlic powder
1 teaspoon sweet cayenne pepper
1 teaspoon hot cayenne pepper
3 teaspoons fine sea salt
2 teaspoons baking powder
400 ml (13½ fl oz) buttermilk
oil for deep-frying

BRINE

1 small onion, thinly sliced
4 garlic cloves, thinly sliced
1 teaspoon vegetable oil
100 g (3½ oz) sea salt
handful of thyme leaves
4 fresh bay leaves
8 peppercorns
1 lemon, quartered
4 regular tea bags

Brine the chicken a day or so ahead. Lightly fry the onion and garlic in the oil in a large saucepan over medium heat, for about 4 minutes. Add the salt, thyme, bay leaves, peppercorns and 1 litre (34 fl oz/4 cups) water. Bring to the boil and stir. When the salt is dissolved, squeeze the lemon quarters in your fist and place them in the brine. Add the tea bags, stir again, then remove from the heat and set aside to cool in a large heatproof bowl. Once cool, place in the fridge to completely chill. As soon as the brine is chilled, remove the tea bags.

Add the chicken pieces to the brine. Weigh the chicken down with a plate that fits inside the bowl, making sure that the chicken is submerged in the brine. Refrigerate for 8–24 hours, agitating the bowl occasionally to ensure that the chicken remains covered by the brine.

Remove the chicken from the brine and rinse under cold water. Pat dry thoroughly with paper towel and set aside on a plate.

Combine the plain flour, polenta, cornflour, spices, sea salt and baking powder in a large bowl. Mix the ingredients thoroughly then divide this mixture between two bowls. Pour the buttermilk into a third bowl.

Working with a few pieces of chicken at a time, lightly coat the pieces, shaking off any excess flour, then dip them in the buttermilk and then back in the flour a second time. Place on a wire rack while you prepare the remainder of the chicken.

Heat the oil in a large saucepan to 180°C (350°F), or until a cube of bread dropped into the oil turns golden in 15 seconds. Cook the chicken, four or five pieces at a time, turning occasionally, until they are cooked through and crisp and golden brown. This will take about 12–15 minutes depending on their size. Remove to a clean wire rack and allow them to drain over paper towel for 5–10 minutes before serving hot.

# BROWN BUTTER ICE CREAM

This is from Simon Bajada's beautiful book, *The New Nordic*. Northern European countries have a long and strong tradition of butter-making and they still produce some of the benchmark butters of the world. Brown butter is butter that has been cooked, caramelising the proteins to give it a sweet, nutty flavour – perfect when made into ice cream.

SERVES 4

100 g (3½ oz) unsalted butter
500 ml (17 fl oz/2 cups) thick (double/heavy) cream
250 ml (8½ fl oz/1 cup) full-cream (whole) milk
6 large egg yolks
80 g (2¾ oz/⅓ cup) caster (superfine) sugar
80 g (2¾ oz/⅓ cup) light brown sugar
1 teaspoon sea salt flakes

Melt the butter in a saucepan over low–medium heat and cook for about 6 minutes or until the butter turns a light amber colour. Be careful not to let it burn. Strain through a fine-meshed sieve into a bowl.

Bring the cream and milk to a simmer in a large saucepan then immediately remove from the heat.

Whisk the egg yolks, both sugars and the salt in a large bowl until thick and well combined. Add the browned butter and whisk together.

Gradually whisk the hot cream mixture into the browned butter mixture, then return to the pan. Stir the mixture over a low–medium heat for 5 minutes, or until it reaches 80°C (175°F). Strain the custard into a clean bowl and set this over a larger bowl filled with ice cubes. Stir, until the custard is chilled.

Churn the custard in an ice-cream machine according to the manufacturer's instructions. Transfer the ice cream to a plastic container and freeze for at least 4 hours before serving.

62

# CROISSANTS

After technique, butter is the most important element to making good croissants. So, use a good one. This recipe takes time and will probably take a couple of goes to get a feel for it, but I guarantee it will bring a little bit of France into your home. The temperature of the butter throughout the process is ultimately what guides the quality of the finished product. Do not let the butter get too soft – work fast and get it back into the fridge.

## MAKES 6

2 teaspoons active dried yeast
2 tablespoons caster (superfine) sugar
170 ml (5½ fl oz) full-cream (whole) milk, at room temperature
290 g (10 oz) plain (all-purpose) flour or bread flour, plus extra for dusting
1 teaspoon salt
170 g (6 oz) chilled unsalted cultured butter
1 egg, beaten

## DAY 1

Combine the yeast, sugar and milk in a large bowl and mix well. Leave it to stand until it starts to look a bit frothy. Tip the flour on top and let sit for 15 minutes until the yeast mixture starts to bubble out the sides of the flour. Add the salt and mix together with a wooden spoon until combined.

Turn the dough out onto a floured work surface and knead until well combined (this should take less than a minute). Place the dough in a clean bowl, cover with plastic wrap and place in the fridge to rest overnight.

## DAY 2

Place the butter between two large pieces of silicone paper and use a rolling pin (and your muscles) to flatten it into a 10 cm x 8 cm (4 in x 3¼ in) rectangle. Return the butter to the fridge to chill for 30 minutes.

Remove the dough from the fridge and roll it out onto a floured work surface into a 25 cm (10 in) square. Place the butter in the centre on a 45 degree angle and fold the corners of the dough over the butter one at a time. (The end result should look a bit like an envelope with the butter inside). Roll the dough into a 30 cm x 20 cm (12 in x 8 in) rectangle. Place the rectangle in front of you with the long edges running left to right. Fold the left side into the centre of the rectangle. Now do the same with the right side. Use your rolling pin to press down several times on the dough to reform a new rectangle (press, rather than roll). Wrap in plastic wrap and chill again for at least 1 hour. Repeat this step two more times.

Roll the dough out again on a lightly floured surface to a neat 30 cm x 20 cm (12 in x 8 in) rectangle. Trim the edges with a sharp knife so that you have a perfect rectangle. With the pastry oriented left to right again, make two cuts to divide the rectangle into three equal rectangles. Now cut each of these rectangles diagonally to form 6 equal triangles.

Start at the wide end of each triangle and roll it up towards the point – it can be pretty loosely rolled. Place the pastries point side up on a baking tray lined with baking paper, ensuring that there is plenty of room between each croissant. Bring the ends together a little to form a crescent shape. Cover with

64

plastic wrap and place the tray in a warm place to prove. The dough should double in size over the next couple of hours.

Preheat the oven to 200°C (400°F). Brush each croissant with a little beaten egg and bake for 10 minutes before reducing the oven temperature to 180°C (350°F), and baking for a further 15–20 minutes until golden brown. Serve warm.

Cressida and Michael McNamara have been milking sheep and making cheese at Pecora Dairy, in Robertson, NSW, since 2005.

# BUTTERMILK SCONES

Buttermilk is slightly sour, which gives a lovely lightness when used in baking. These scones are fantastic served with cream and passionfruit butter.

MAKES 12

525 g (1 lb 3 oz/3½ cups)
  self-raising flour, plus
  extra for dusting
2 tablespoons caster
  (superfine) sugar
pinch of salt
60 g (2 oz) unsalted butter,
  chopped
375 ml (12½ fl oz/1½ cups)
  cultured buttermilk
Passionfruit Butter (see
  below) and whipped
  cream, to serve

Preheat the oven to 200°C (400°F). Line a baking tray with baking paper.

Combine the flour, sugar and salt in a large bowl. Add the butter and work it through the flour using your fingertips, until it resembles breadcrumbs. Add the buttermilk and mix together with a metal spoon (be careful not to over-mix).

Turn the mixture out onto a lightly floured work surface and quickly and lightly knead to form a dough. Use your hands to press it into a flat disc about 3 cm (1¼ in) thick. Use a 5 cm (2 in) biscuit (cookie) cutter to cut out rounds. Knead the scraps back into a flat shape and repeat until all the dough is used.

Place the scones on the baking tray and bake for 15 minutes or until golden. Serve warm with passionfruit butter and cream.

# PASSIONFRUIT BUTTER

Passionfruit butter is big in my childhood memory of tastes. My nana used to make it, and I can remember finding a cupboard full of it stored in recycled Kraft Cheese Spread jars (I never said she was perfect). These days, to sound more fancy, we call it passionfruit 'curd' and it can make pavlova posh, scones sinful and ice cream incredible.

MAKES ABOUT 250 G
(9 OZ/1 CUP)

125 g (4½ oz) chilled unsalted
  cultured butter, chopped
150 g (5½ oz) caster
  (superfine) sugar
180 ml (6 fl oz) fresh
  passionfruit pulp
4 egg yolks

Combine the butter, sugar and passionfruit pulp in a medium-sized saucepan and melt over low heat. Add the egg yolks (making sure there is no egg white) and stir to combine. Cook, stirring constantly, for 10–15 minutes or until the mixture thickens and coats the back of a spoon. Do not let it boil.

Remove from the heat, stir for 5 minutes as the mixture cools then transfer to a sterilised glass jar and place in the fridge for 1 hour to chill.

The butter will store well in your fridge for several weeks.

# BUTTER SHORTBREAD

This is the real thing – fat fingers of super short and buttery shortbread.

MAKES ABOUT 12 FINGERS

350 g (12½ oz/2⅓ cups) plain (all-purpose) flour, plus extra for dusting

145 g (5 oz/⅔ cup) caster (superfine) sugar, plus extra for sprinkling

230 g (8 oz) chilled unsalted cultured butter, cut into cubes

Preheat the oven to 160°C (320°F). Line a baking tray with baking paper.

Mix the flour and sugar in a large bowl. Add the butter and work it through the flour using your fingertips, until it resembles coarse breadcrumbs.

Turn the mixture out onto a lightly dusted work surface, and quickly knead to form a smooth dough ball. Roll the dough into a rectangle about 2 cm (¾ in) thick. Carefully lift onto the baking tray. Using a sharp knife, score the surface about 3–4 mm (¼ in) deep into fat finger shapes. Sprinkle the surface with caster sugar.

Bake in the oven for 20–30 minutes until pale golden. Be careful not overcook or the shortbread will be dry. Cool on a wire rack and store in an airtight container for up to 2 weeks.

# YOGHURT

Even though yoghurt, like cheese, has undergone fermentation, the curds are not separated from the whey like they are in cheese; instead, the milk remains whole.

Finding great yoghurt is becoming harder and harder. Most commercial yoghurts contain thickeners, sweeteners, milk powder, preservatives and colours. I never fail to be impressed by how we are able to stuff up even the purest and simplest foods. The good news is that making great yoghurt at home is as simple as falling off a log. As long as you have access to good milk, with some basic techniques your home-made yoghurt will be better than anything you can buy.

It seems that almost every culture that has used milk has featured yoghurt in its cuisine. The making, eating and cooking of yoghurt has been recorded in written history from India to Persia and from Pliny the Elder's *Natural History* to the *Old Testament*.

Yoghurt is basically fermented milk. The basic principle is to first heat the milk to 85°C (185°F). This has two effects: first, it denatures the proteins in the milk and causes them to bind together as the milk cools and ferments, giving the yoghurt its thick texture; and secondly, it kills off the naturally occurring bacteria in the milk, providing a competition-free environment for the introduced yoghurt bacteria to thrive. If you are a hard-core raw milk fanatic, you can make 'raw' yoghurt by not heating the milk, but this will produce a thinner texture and give inconsistent results, as it allows any bacteria present in the milk to grow.

The bacteria used to make commercial yoghurt, generally a combination of *Lactobacillus bulgaricus* and *Streptococcus thermophilus*, both occur naturally in milk and are used to produce the beautiful acidity and texture of yoghurt. The better varieties of yoghurt have a nutritional value greater than the milk from which they are made due to the probiotic nature of 'live' yoghurt.

Milk with a high percentage of milk solids, such as sheep's milk or buffalo's milk, makes the thickest, richest yoghurt. Commercial yoghurt made from cow's milk often has milk powder added to boost the milk solids and thicken the texture.

### Kefir

Kefir is a fermented, cultured milk product with a long history. It is thicker than milk and runnier than yoghurt and can be super acidic and even slightly fizzy. Unlike yoghurt, the fermentative culture is a complex biology that includes yeasts and bacteria in a symbiotic relationship that forms whitish grains or 'crystals'. These unique biological ecosystems are self-perpetuating and will not only ferment the lactose in milk to lactic acid but will also convert small amounts of alcohol in the process.

You will need to acquire some kefir grains if you want to make it at home. Ask at your local wholefoods store. After that, it is simply a matter of adding about 5% kefir grains to 95% milk in a sterilised jar or bottle. It does not require any heating and can be made at room temperature. Your kefir will be ready after a day or so, after it has thickened slightly. The kefir grains can be strained, rinsed and reused.

# HOW TO MAKE YOGHURT

This yoghurt is made using cow's milk, so I have included a straining step to achieve the thicker texture familiar to most yoghurts; however, you don't need to strain it if you prefer a thinner style. It's important to try and get good milk – ideally super fresh, raw milk. If you don't have a cow in your backyard, or are friends with someone who does, packaged milk is fine as long as it is unhomogenised. You will also need a thermometer and a home-made 'incubator' before you begin (see below).

**MAKES 1.5 KG (3 LB 5 OZ/ 6 CUPS)**

1.5 litres (51 fl oz/6 cups) full-cream (whole) milk

3–4 teaspoons 'live' natural yoghurt

Heat the milk in a large saucepan over medium heat to 85°C (185°F), using a sugar thermometer to assist you. Stir regularly with a stainless steel slotted spoon to stop the milk from catching on the bottom.

Transfer the saucepan to a sink half-filled with cold water. Stir the milk until the temperature lowers to around 35°C (95°F).

Pour the cooled milk into sterilised glass jars. Stir a few teaspoons of live yoghurt into each jar. Stir each jar for a couple of minutes to make sure the yoghurt is well distributed.

Place your jars in your 'incubator' (see below) and leave undisturbed for a minimum of 8 hours, after which the yoghurt should be completely set. If it is still runny, return it to the incubator at 45°C (113°F) for another 4 hours. At this point the yoghurt is ready to eat, but if you prefer it a bit thicker pour it into a colander lined with a few layers of rinsed muslin (cheesecloth) and leave to drain for 1 hour. Spoon the yoghurt into a clean sterilised jar, seal with the lid and store in the fridge for up to 10 days.

If the yoghurt has turned out well, set aside a few spoonfuls to use as your next starter culture. As long as you continue to make yoghurt at least once a week your culture will stay alive. This means that every subsequent batch becomes more of your own unique yoghurt.

This plain yoghurt is wonderful on its own or in savoury dishes. If you want to sweeten it, add a little honey or a spoonful of jam.

### Incubator

To make the yoghurt you need to keep the temperature of the milk ideally between 43°C–45°C (109°F–113°F) for 8–12 hours. This can be achieved in several ways: you can put the milk in the oven with the pilot light left on, or on a very low setting with the door slightly ajar; or place in a small cooler or polystyrene box with a warming lamp. You may need to be a little bit creative and try a few different options before you get it right.

# LABNEH

I adore yoghurt and the clean smack of lemony acid that comes with it. Labneh is basically yoghurt with some of the moisture removed. The result is a thick, versatile fresh cheese that can be eaten straight up or marinated and stored. Allowed to mature it becomes the funky and pungent Middle Eastern cheese called shankleesh (see page 78).

First of all let's talk about which yoghurt to use. The best is plain pot-set yoghurt. Greek yoghurt is OK, but check the ingredients to make sure it does not contain gelatine or any thickening agents or gums. Most Greek cow's milk yoghurt will have extra protein added to beef it up (usually in the form of milk powder). This will give you a better yield but not as nice a texture. Sheep's, goat's or buffalo milk yoghurt is naturally thicker. Alternatively, try making your own yoghurt (see page 75).

**MAKES ABOUT 700 G (1 LB 9 OZ)**

1 kg (2 lb 3 oz) plain pot-set yoghurt

Line a colander with two layers of rinsed muslin (cheesecloth). Spoon the yoghurt into the muslin and tie the corners together to make a bag. Slide a wooden spoon under the knot and hang it over the edge of the colander so that the bag is suspended. Set aside in the fridge to drain, set over a bowl to catch the drips.

The longer you leave it, the thicker the labneh will be. It will stop draining after about 72 hours, at which stage it will be very firm. If you are after a softer texture, drain it for 12–24 hours only. Labneh will only keep for a few days in the fridge but can be preserved in oil to extend its life (see below).

WHAT TO DO WITH LABNEH:
- Roll into small balls and carefully pack in a sterilised glass jar. Add a few cloves of garlic and some fresh herbs and cover with olive oil. It will keep for up to three weeks.
- Use as an accompaniment to curries and aromatic tagines.
- Blend with fresh herbs or spices and olive oil to make a dip.
- Sweeten it with honey and vanilla to serve with sweet tarts or fresh berries.
- Turn it into shankleesh (see page 78).

76

# SHANKLEESH

Shankleesh is a bit of a mystery to me. In the Middle East you will find it in all sorts of forms, but basically it is labneh that has been allowed to age and then rolled in spices. It can look pretty horrible but tastes amazing! The real stuff can be pretty hard to find outside of the Middle East but the following recipe will get you pretty close.

MAKES 500 G (1 LB 2 OZ)

500 g (1lb 2 oz) labneh, drained for at least 48 hours and quite firm (see page 76)
1 tablespoon za'atar
1 tablespoon sumac
1 teaspoon ground aniseed
1 teaspoon chilli flakes
1 teaspoon freshly ground black pepper
2 teaspoons salt
4 teaspoons dried oregano
2 teaspoons dried mint

Mix the labneh, spices and salt together and form into two balls. Mix the oregano and the mint together on a plate and roll the labneh balls in the herbs until completely covered.

Place the balls of labneh in a clean, airtight plastic container and store in the fridge for 5–7 days.

Use shankleesh as an accompaniment to soups or stews, crumble it over salads or just eat it with a drizzle of strong olive oil and some crusty bread.

# YOGHURT SOUP WITH CHICKEN AND RICE

This is SO good! I ate something similar to this years ago at a terrific restaurant in Adelaide called Mona Lisa's. It was a restaurant I visited in my early years and it helped shape my love for food and the theatre that can be so effortless yet seductive in good restaurants. This soup is a meal in itself.

SERVES 6

1 litre (34 fl oz/4 cups) chicken stock
400 g (14 oz) free-range skinless boneless chicken thighs, cut into small cubes
300 g (10½ oz) plain yoghurt
2 tablespoons plain (all-purpose) flour
1 large egg yolk
185 g (6½ oz/1 cup) cooked basmati rice
400 g (14 oz) tinned chickpeas, drained
1 tablespoon extra-virgin olive oil
2 tablespoons butter
3 garlic cloves, finely chopped
2 teaspoons sweet paprika
1 teaspoon ground cumin
1 teaspoon ground coriander
½ teaspoon freshly ground black pepper
big pinch of cayenne pepper
3 tablespoons finely chopped mint leaves
1 tablespoon finely chopped oregano leaves

Bring the stock to the boil in a medium-sized saucepan, then reduce the heat to a simmer. Add the chicken, cover and cook for about 10 minutes or until cooked through. Remove the chicken using a slotted spoon and set aside. Remove the stock from the heat and set aside.

In another saucepan, whisk the yoghurt, flour and egg yolk over low heat until thoroughly combined. Add the hot stock one ladle at a time and continue to whisk. Once all the stock is incorporated, add the rice, chickpeas and cooked chicken. Keep on a low heat and do not allow to boil.

Heat the oil, butter, garlic and spices in a frying pan until the butter melts, then remove from the heat.

Mix together the mint and oregano in a small bowl.

Divide the soup among four bowls and serve drizzled with a spoonful of the melted spiced butter and a sprinkle of the herbs.

80

# SHISH BARAK

Shish barak are Lebanese meat dumplings cooked in yoghurt. Strangely, the first time I ate this dish was not in Lebanon, but on Bruny Island, cooked by a seventh-generation Tasmanian (albeit a really good chef who had cooked in Europe for 20 years before returning home). This dish is a bit of effort but the results are intoxicating. Make extra dumplings, dust them in flour and freeze for up to one month.

SERVES 4

500 g (1 lb 2 oz/2 cups)
    plain yoghurt
1 egg
1 tablespoon plain
    (all-purpose) flour
2 garlic cloves, finely chopped
½ teaspoon dried mint
½ teaspoon dried coriander
½ teaspoon dried oregano
½ teaspoon salt
juice of 1 lemon
olive oil, for drizzling

MEAT FILLING

2 tablespoons olive oil
1 small onion, grated
250 g (9 oz) minced (ground)
    lean beef
¼ teaspoon ground cloves
¼ teaspoon ground cinnamon
¼ teaspoon ground nutmeg
¼ teaspoon ground coriander
¼ teaspoon white pepper
¼ teaspoon freshly ground
    black pepper
½ teaspoon sea salt
40 g (1½ oz/¼ cup) pine nuts

DUMPLING DOUGH

¼ teaspoon active dry yeast
pinch of sugar
300 g (10½ oz/2 cups) plain
    (all-purpose) flour, plus
    extra for dusting
1 teaspoon sea salt

To make the meat filling, heat the olive oil in a heavy-based frying pan over medium heat, and sauté the onion for a few minutes. Add the beef, spices and salt and continue to cook, stirring occasionally, until the beef is browned and cooked through. Stir through the pine nuts and cook for a few more minutes until any remaining moisture has evaporated. Set aside to cool.

To make the dumpling dough, mix the yeast, 60 ml (2 fl oz/¼ cup) warm water and the sugar together in a cup and set aside for a few minutes to activate the yeast. Once the yeast mixture looks foamy, put it in a food processor along with the flour, 300 ml (10 fl oz) cold water and the salt and process to form a soft dough. Turn out onto a well floured work surface and knead with your hands for a few minutes until the dough is smooth and firm but not stiff. Add a little more flour if the dough feels wet and sticky.

Roll the dough out to about 3 mm (⅛ in) thick, keeping the dough well dusted with flour. Use a 3–4 cm (1¼–1½ in) biscuit (cookie) cutter to cut out discs. Roll out any remaining scraps of dough until it is all used (you should have about 30 discs).

Place half a teaspoon of meat filling in the centre of one disc then pull two opposite sides of the dough circle together and press lightly to seal. Bring the remaining two sides of the circle to the middle and pinch the edges together with a dab of water to form a star-shaped dumpling. Place the finished dumpling on a plate dusted with flour. Repeat this process until all the discs and filling are used.

To make the shish barak, place the yoghurt, 250 ml (8½ fl oz/1 cup) water and the egg and flour in a heavy-based saucepan and stir with a whisk until well combined. Bring to a gentle simmer over a low heat, stirring constantly to ensure that the mixture does not curdle. Add the garlic, dried herbs and salt and stir. Add the lemon juice and stir again. Simmer for a couple of minutes then add the dumplings, bring to a gentle boil and reduce to a simmer for 20 minutes or until the dumplings are cooked through.

Serve hot, in bowls, drizzled with olive oil.

# BENGALI YOGHURT FISH CURRY

I am a sucker for a good fish curry. It's about the only time I do anything to fish other than cook it really simply. In Bengal they call this Doi Maach and they generally use chunks of freshwater fish, but it is great with almost any firm fish that does not fall apart.

SERVES 4

1 medium onion, roughly chopped, and 1 large onion, finely chopped
1 red chilli, deseeded and roughly chopped
4 garlic cloves, roughly chopped
2 cm (¾ in) piece fresh ginger, peeled and roughly chopped
250 g (9 oz/1 cup) plain yoghurt
½ teaspoon turmeric powder
½ teaspoon chilli powder
1 kg (2 lb 3 oz) firm white fish fillets, cut into chunks
4 tablespoons ghee
1½ teaspoons curry powder
4 cloves
5 black peppercorns
4 green cardamom pods
2 cm (¾ in) cinnamon stick
1 tablespoon dried curry leaves
1 dried bay leaf
cooked basmati rice, to serve

In a food processor or with a mortar and pestle, process or pound the roughly chopped onion, chilli, garlic and ginger to a paste. Combine the yoghurt, turmeric and chilli powder in a large bowl and add the onion mixture. Add the fish pieces and gently mix to coat well. Cover the bowl with plastic wrap and marinate in the fridge for 2–4 hours.

Heat the ghee in a deep heavy-based saucepan over medium heat. Add the remaining spices and bay leaf, and fry for about 2 minutes or until lightly browned. Add the finely chopped onion and fry for a further 2 minutes, stirring constantly.

Add the marinated fish and all of the marinade to the pan and stir gently while bringing to the boil. Reduce the heat immediately to a low simmer and cook for about 10 minutes, or until the fish is cooked through. You can add a splash of water if it is too dry.

Serve hot with basmati rice.

# WALLABY KOFTA WITH CACIK

In Tasmania, where I live, wallabies are native and their meat is available from most butchers' shops. It might not be as traditional as lamb, but wallaby kofta tastes easily as good. Cacik is a Turkish dish similar to tzatziki – it is served alongside the meal and eaten cold with a spoon, or used to accompany grilled meats, as in this recipe.

SERVES 6–8
flatbreads, to serve (optional)

CACIK
2 tablespoons extra-virgin
    olive oil
500 g (1 lb 2 oz/ 2 cups) plain
    yoghurt (goat's milk yoghurt
    is preferable but any good
    plain yoghurt is fine)
2 medium cucumbers,
    peeled and coarsely grated
1 teaspoon sea salt
½ teaspoon white pepper
3 garlic cloves, finely chopped
2 tablespoons finely chopped
    mint leaves
2 teaspoons finely chopped
    flat-leaf parsley leaves
2 teaspoons finely chopped
    oregano leaves

KOFTA
700 g (1 lb 9 oz) minced
    (ground) wallaby or lamb
1 egg
1 small onion, grated
1 teaspoon ground cumin
1 teaspoon salt
2 teaspoons ground coriander
2 garlic cloves, finely chopped
1 tablespoon finely chopped
    mint leaves
1 tablespoon finely chopped
    flat-leaf parsley leaves
vegetable oil for brushing

To make the cacik, whisk the olive oil, yoghurt and 60 ml (2 fl oz/¼ cup) cold water in a medium-sized bowl. Add the remaining ingredients and stir until well combined. Cover with plastic wrap and chill in the fridge for a couple of hours to let the flavours mingle.

Preheat your barbecue or grill (broiler) to very hot.

To make the kofta, use your hands to mix all of the ingredients together in a large bowl. Divide the mixture into 12 even-sized balls, then thread 2 balls each onto metal skewers and squeeze to form sausage shapes. Brush the koftas with oil then place on the barbecue and cook for about 4 minutes on each side or until cooked through. Serve with cacik and flatbreads (if desired).

Cacik can be stored in an airtight container in the fridge for up to a week (but the garlic will get more potent the longer you leave it).

Cows at Sugar House Creamery, in Upper Jay, New York, are milked straight into the churn. The milk is then strained and chilled before being made into cheese.

# YOGHURT-MARINATED BARBECUE CHICKEN

This is great barbecue fare. It is a take on the classic tandoori chicken but with less of an Indian influence. Make sure your barbecue is smokin' hot to get a bit of caramelisation happening on the outside of the chicken. You can marinate the chicken up to a day ahead. Serve with salad or in a bun with some slaw for the ultimate chicken burger.

SERVES 6

560 g (1 lb 4 oz/2¼ cups)
    plain yoghurt
100 ml (3½ fl oz) good quality
    olive oil
2½ tablespoons freshly
    squeezed lime juice
3 teaspoons sea salt
1 tablespoon cayenne pepper
1 teaspoon chilli flakes
¾ teaspoon ground cumin
¾ teaspoon ground coriander
2 garlic cloves, finely
    chopped
12 free-range boneless
    chicken thighs, skin on

Mix all of the ingredients, except the chicken, together in a large bowl. Add the chicken thighs, mix well, cover with plastic wrap and place in the fridge for 2–12 hours.

Preheat your barbecue to very hot.

Remove the chicken from the fridge and, using tongs, scrape each thigh on the edge of the bowl to remove the bulk of the yoghurt marinade. Place the chicken thighs on the barbecue and cook for 6–8 minutes on each side, until cooked through.

90

# HONEY, LEMON AND CARDAMOM FROZEN YOGHURT

Frozen yoghurt shops are spreading across the planet like wildfire. And for good reason, frozen yoghurt tastes great and it is a healthier option than a daily bowl of ice cream (unless, of course, you top it with chocolate-covered honeycomb or highly sweetened fruit). It has a milder taste and texture than traditional ice cream. The important thing is to eat it quickly, as the texture disintegrates within a day or two of being made.

**MAKES ABOUT 1.5 LITRES (51 FL OZ/6 CUPS)**

125 ml (4 fl oz/½ cup) full-cream (whole) milk

115 g (4 oz/½ cup) caster (superfine) sugar

10 green cardamom pods, coarsely chopped

175 g (6 oz/½ cup) honey, warmed

1 vanilla bean, split and seeds scraped

zest of 1 lemon

1 kg (2 lb 3 oz/4 cups) plain yoghurt

2 teaspoons lemon juice

Heat the milk, sugar, cardamom, honey, vanilla bean and seeds and lemon zest in a small saucepan over medium heat and stir until the sugar and honey are dissolved. Strain the mixture into a large bowl, discarding the vanilla bean, cardamom pods and any lemon zest that gets caught in the sieve. Set aside to cool completely.

Stir in the yoghurt and lemon juice with a whisk, then transfer to an ice cream machine and churn according to the manufacturer's instructions.

Unlike custard-based ice cream, you can serve frozen yoghurt straight from the churn, but I prefer to give it a blast in the freezer for a couple of hours first to firm up a bit.

# SHRIKHAND

India has a sweet tooth that spans the country and goes back thousands of years in its history. The word sugar even comes from the Sanskrit language. Many Indian sweets use milk, paneer or yoghurt as their base. Shrikhand is super easy to make and the perfect way to finish a curry, but you need to make it a day ahead to drain the yoghurt.

SERVES 6

1 kg (2 lb 3 oz/4 cups) plain yoghurt

pinch of saffron threads, steeped in 1 tablespoon boiling water

6 green cardamom pods, seeds removed and crushed

1 tablespoon rosewater

110 g (4 oz/½ cup) caster (superfine) sugar

2 tablespoons raw pistachio nuts, chopped

Line a colander with two layers of rinsed, fine muslin (cheesecloth). Spoon the yoghurt into the muslin and tie the corners together to form a bag. Slide a wooden spoon under the knot and hang it over the edge of the colander so that the bag is suspended. Set aside in the fridge to drain, set over a bowl to catch the drips, for 12–18 hours.

Scrape the yoghurt into a bowl. Add the saffron water, cardamom, rosewater, sugar and half the pistachios. Beat the mixture with a spoon until light and fluffy.

Serve in small bowls, topped with the remaining pistachios.

# ICELANDIC SKYR, HONEY AND CINNAMON CAKE

---

If I didn't live in Tasmania I would want to live in Iceland. I have only been there once but have been utterly smitten ever since. Iceland to me is like that kid we all went to school with – the one that was a total individual, so cool and self-confident it was impossible not to marvel at them from afar, drooling with jealous admiration, mystified by how they were so different, when everybody else was at pains to be the same as each other. Now I read Icelandic literature, listen to their music and try and cook their food. I want to be Icelandic. I have become Iceland's stalker and in my eyes they can do no wrong.

Take this cake, for example. Anywhere else in the world and it would just be a no-bake cheesecake. But this is from Iceland, using skyr, a kind of Icelandic yoghurt. So it's awesome.

SERVES 10

8 gelatine sheets
500 g (1 lb 2 oz) plain skyr
    or quark
2 eggs
85 g (3 oz) honey, warmed,
    plus extra, for drizzling
1 vanilla bean, split and
    seeds scraped
1 teaspoon ground cinnamon
2 tablespoons caster
    (superfine) sugar
250 ml (8½ fl oz/1 cup) thick
    (double/heavy) cream
80 ml (2½ fl oz/⅓ cup)
    full-cream (whole) milk
fresh figs, quartered, to serve

BASE

200 g (7 oz) dates, pitted
100 g (3½ oz) shredded
    coconut
200 g (7 oz) almond meal

Grease and line the base and side of a 25 cm (10 in) springform cake tin with silicone paper.

Make the base by processing all of the ingredients in a food processor until they come together to form a moist breadcrumb-like mixture. Add a little boiling water to soften if required (some dates are dryer than others). Press the date mixture evenly into the bottom of the cake tin using your fingers or the back of a spoon. Place in the fridge to firm up while you make the filling.

In a small bowl, soften the gelatine in some hot water.

Combine the skyr, eggs, honey, vanilla seeds and cinnamon in a large bowl. In the bowl of an electric mixer, whisk the sugar and cream together until peaks are formed and the sugar is dissolved. Fold this into the skyr mixture.

Squeeze the water out of the softened gelatine sheets and place in a small saucepan with the milk. Over a low heat, stir until the gelatine is completely dissolved. Allow to cool, then stir into the skyr and cream mixture until combined. Spoon the mixture over the cake base and smooth the top with a spatula.

Cover with plastic wrap and chill in the fridge for 8 hours. Drizzle with warmed honey and top with the fresh figs just before serving.

# SUGAR HOUSE CREAMERY

Alex Eaton and Margot Brooks are dedicated to their craft. Rarely do you see an operation so impressive, from the way they care for their twelve Brown Swiss cows and their dedication to producing exceptional raw milk and raw milk cheese, to their commitment to replenishing their community and environment. It all made me want to be a better cheesemaker. And a better person.

Sugar House Creamery (named because the main barn formerly produced maple syrup) is in Upper Jay, New York, in the stunning Adirondack Mountains. Margot grew up on a multi-generational dairy farm, where she and partner Alex saw their future. They wanted to continue milking but also add a creamery to produce cheese and add value to the milk, but couldn't make it happen within the family structure. So, in 2012 they bought their own 23 acre (9 hectare) farm.

It was run down and required loads of work. The soil was depleted and the buildings all needed fixing up. They converted an existing barn into a milking parlour, cheesemaking facility and cave. The barn stores hay in the loft, which is dropped through a hole in the floor straight into the milking parlour. The cows are pastured as much as possible in the summer and spring but are housed in the barn throughout the colder months.

The morning I arrived, the cows were already being milked. It was early winter, and there was about a foot of snow on the ground and the sun was not yet up. The cows are milked straight into a small stainless-steel milk churn, and the milk is then poured through a filter into a small cooling vat. As soon as milking is finished, the chilled milk is decanted into sterilised 2 litre (½ gallon) jars which are loaded onto a hand trolley and wheeled 25 metre (80 feet) to their Farm Store where they're placed directly in the fridge – raw milk, straight from cow to the consumer in under 60 minutes! The milk from Brown Swiss cows is more naturally homogenised than that of other breeds – you don't get the thick layer of cream rising to the top like you would with, say, Jersey milk.

In their tiny cave that lies beneath their tiny cheesemaking room, Margot tells me about the farm.

Margot and Alex form the curd for their Dutch Knuckle under the whey, ready to be hooped.

The cave is set 1.5 m (5 ft) below ground level to achieve a constant temperature between 8°C–15°C (46°F–59°F). It has a beautiful vaulted ceiling (a design picked up from the couple's time spent at another local dairy and cheesemaker, Consider Bardwell Farm) which prevents condensation dripping from the ceiling; instead it just runs down the walls.

## WHAT ROUTINE DO YOU GO THROUGH EVERY TIME YOU ENTER HERE?

*The first thing I do is smell – the first sense to light up is always smell. Then I look at the floor, is it wet? Or dry? That will tell me how humid it is. We don't measure humidity – we just feel it. Then I feel the temperature. Do I need to warm it or cool it? Then I feel the air movement to make sure there is enough fresh air (air intake is 60 metres/200 feet away so that the air is cooled on the way in).*

## WHAT THINGS DID YOU PLACE MOST IMPORTANCE ON WHEN SETTING UP THE FARM AND CREAMERY?

*The barn, the vat and the cave; they were the three big investments we made. We could have gone much cheaper*

*on all of them but we really felt strongly about hitting the ground with a good product. They are our main tools that enable us to really drive quality into our products. The cave was important because we wanted to make natural-rinded cheese, and the only way to do that is in a cave like ours. It was designed to age Dutch Knuckle for 6 months, but when we started making it we much preferred it at 9 months, which means the cave is always full and we are always pushed for space.*

## WHY DID YOU CHOOSE BROWN SWISS COWS?

*They are not a common breed in the US but we like them because they are big and strong and have very gentle personalities. The milk also suited the type of cheese we wanted to make.*

## ULTIMATELY, WHAT DRIVES YOU?

*Our satisfaction comes from the feeling that our efforts are making a difference; not from winning awards or seeing our cheeses on menus at restaurants, but from improving our own little piece of land and seeing our neighbours leave our farm store loaded up with milk and cheese.*

Dutch Knuckle, a raw milk cooked curd
cheese aged for six to nine months.

# CHEESE

To me, making cheese is a wondrous, transformative alchemy. It's about preserving a moment in time; a moment which reflects the provenance of the milk, the type and breed of the animal, what the animal has eaten and the microclimate and geography of the environment in which it lives. This is the terroir of the cheese; its unique characteristics and its personality.

Making cheese is way more complicated than following a recipe. It is not like baking a cake. Cheese is made as much in the paddock and the maturation room as it is in the vat.

**Preparation of the milk**
Depending on the cheese being made, its country of origin and the preference of the cheesemaker, the milk may be pasteurised. This is a heat treatment used to kill pathogenic bacteria. The standard time/temperature ratio is to bring the milk to 72°C (162°F) and hold it for 15 seconds, and then cool it quickly to prevent further damage to the milk. In a small cheesery, this is often done on a batch basis where a vat of milk is brought up to temperature en masse and then cooled en masse. Turning the temperature around quickly is difficult with a large quantity of liquid so batch pasteurisation may happen at a lower temperature and held for longer (such as 68°C/154°F for 4 minutes). The lower the temperature used, the less of the milk's natural, beneficial microbiology will be destroyed along with the bad bugs. The good bacteria contribute to the natural flavour and character of the milk. This is why raw milk cheeses (which have received no heat treatment at all) are said to have better flavour than pasteurised cheeses.

The reason for pasteurisation is to destroy any pathogenic bacteria that might be present in the milk. In countries such as Australia, mandatory pasteurisation laws are imposed on cheesemakers and farmers. This is based on the false assumption that all milk contains pathogenic bacteria. This assumption is not only ignorant, but also dangerous. Super fresh milk that has come from healthy animals that have been fed well and treated humanely, and has been chilled quickly and handled minimally, is fundamentally a safe product. It also contains all of the good bacteria needed for cheesemaking.

In big cheese factories the milk, which is collected from many different farms and pooled together, is often fiddled with to achieve a standard quality, because large-scale producers are looking for a highly consistent end product that does not differ throughout the year with the change in seasons. This might involve adding or removing components such as cream, protein, lactose or calcium.

These factories may also replace pasteurisation with a process called ultra-filtration, which ruins the natural texture of the milk and produces rubbish cheese. Smaller, more traditional cheese producers are happy to let these seasonal variations come through in their cheeses and tell the story of how and when they were made.

Regardless of whether the milk is heat-treated or not, it still needs to be brought to a temperature that is favourable for the lactic acid bacteria to thrive. Depending on the type of cheese being made, this is generally between 28°C– 38°C (82°F–100°F).

## Fermentation

Bacterial starter cultures are the gatekeepers to modern, commercial cheesemaking. They are also the executioner of traditional cheeses and true flavour. Commercial bacterial cultures not only give modern, mass-produced cheese its desired flavour, but they also acidify the milk, which helps to preserve the cheese as well as playing a vital role in the coagulation of the curd. These cultures all comprise lactic acid–producing bacteria (derived from milk and reproduced in commercial laboratories). The bacteria feed on the naturally occurring lactose in the milk and convert it into lactic acid, thus increasing the acidity of the milk, which assists in coagulation and preservation of the cheese. Rapid development of acidity in cheesemaking is important, especially in raw milk cheeses, as lactic acid-producing bacteria can suppress any disease-producing bacteria that might be present.

There are many different types of lactic acid-producing bacteria, all of which contribute unique characteristics to cheese. Each type of bacteria will be most active at a certain temperature: mesophilic bacteria, for example, used for fresh, soft and semi-hard cheeses, operates best between 30°C–37°C (86°F–99°F); thermophilic bacteria, however, prefers a higher temperature of 38+°C (100+°F) and is used in hard, cooked curd cheeses where the temperature increase helps to dry out the curd.

Modern starter cultures are available in all sorts of single strains or blends of bacteria, and are usually in freeze-dried or frozen form. Cheesemakers select the right mix of bacteria for the type of cheese being made and add them directly to the cheese vat to inoculate the milk. These starter cultures are largely the reason that traditional cheeses can now be made anywhere in the world. Commercial starter cultures reduce the risk of cheesemaking faults and defects, but they also homogenise the flavour and character of real cheese.

Like any form of fermentation, cheesemaking is a very natural process. It is one which we have managed to complicate and compromise in the interests of protecting ourselves from perceived or imagined threats to our safety or to increase efficiency. Traditional cheesemakers not only use raw milk to initiate fermentation, with its natural bacterial ecology intact, they often also use whey starters by seeding their milk with some of the previous day's whey and introducing the specific bacteria of their herd and location, similar to the way a baker uses part of the previous day's dough to make a new batch of bread. Cheeses made this way are rare as hen's teeth in the New World and even in countries such as France and Italy, it is becoming harder to make cheese like this.

## Coagulation

Coagulation is the process of turning liquid milk into a solid state. Using the word 'solid' might be overstating it a bit as the texture of coagulated milk is similar to a jelly. In fact, the olden-days dessert junket – a kind of milk pudding with the texture of blancmange – was really just milk that had been coagulated with the same stuff that cheesemakers use to make cheese. Coagulation is the basis of cheesemaking – it is what sets it apart from other fermented dairy products such as yoghurt. There are two types of coagulation: lactic coagulation and rennet coagulation, although they are sometimes used in conjunction with each other in order to obtain consistent results.

Lactic coagulation occurs when the naturally present lactic acid-producing bacteria are able to thrive in the correct conditions and produce enough acidity to change the nature of the casein present and coagulate the milk. In fact, we have all had a go at lactic coagulation – when you leave a carton of milk out of the fridge and it goes lumpy, that's lactic coagulation. The acidity increases, and the milk protein curdles. Lactic coagulation takes longer (up to 24 hours) than rennet coagulation and produces fragile, more porous curds, which are excellent for cheeses that require a delicate texture. Most of the fresh and soft goat's cheeses from France use lactic coagulation to achieve their beautiful, fudge-like texture.

105

Rennet coagulation relies on an enzyme called rennin to change the structure of the casein present so that it forms a matrix and, therefore, coagulates the milk. Rennet coagulation happens in a fraction of the time as lactic coagulation (3–60 minutes) and produces curds which are denser, firmer and more elastic than lactic curds – perfect for semi-hard and hard cheeses. Cow's milk cheeses generally use rennet coagulation because they contain lower quantities of milk solids.

There are three types of rennet:

**Animal rennet:** made since the 16th century and involves the extraction of enzymes from the stomachs of calves, lambs or goats. The most traditional cheeses still add a dried, or even fresh piece of the stomach directly to the milk in the cheesemaking vat. These cheeses are obviously not suitable for vegetarians as the enzyme is taken from the animal after it has been killed.

**Microbial rennet:** produced by artificial synthesis of the rennin enzyme. This is mostly achieved by growing the enzyme on a mould (usually common mucor). It is good for vegetarians.

**Vegetable rennet:** extracted from certain plants, including figs, artichokes and cardoons (a type of edible thistle); however, in my experience this is pretty rare, quite expensive to buy and woefully unpredictable to use.

### Cutting and stirring the curds

After coagulation the milk solids are held in a gel-like matrix that binds together the protein and fat and traps the liquid whey within it. Cutting this matrix up allows the whey to escape, leaving behind the milk solids, or curd. The more the curd is cut, the greater the surface area available for the whey to escape. Therefore, the finer the curd, the drier the cheese. As a crude example, brie curd is cut to the size of golf balls, whereas cheddar curd is cut to the size of peas, and the curd of hard cheeses such as Parmigiano Reggiano is cut to the size of lentils. After cutting, the casein exposed by the cut surface wants to knit the curd back together – stirring keeps the curds separate until the cut surfaces have formed a 'skin', which helps prevent the curds from reforming. After cutting, the curds remain in the whey where they are stirred and often heated until the desired level of acidity and moisture is achieved.

### Heating the curds

While suspended in whey, curds are sometimes heated up to 50°C (122°F). This step is most common in harder cheeses, called cooked curd cheeses, as the heating results in the curd particles shrinking and expelling more whey, resulting in a drier cheese. The remaining lactose in the whey will also start to 'caramelise' at temperatures of 47°C (117°F) or more, producing sweet, nutty flavours in the cheese.

### Draining and hooping

The separated curd is transferred to 'hoops' or 'moulds' (hoops are usually straight-sided, cylindrical, perforated containers that mould and form the cheese and dictate its final shape and size). In the case of fresh and soft cheeses, the hoops are then, placed on a flat surface for the remaining whey to drain or, in the case of some hard cheeses, placed in a press to force the remaining whey out of the curds. The cheese is turned regularly to aid even drainage.

### Salting

Salt is vital to cheesemaking. The addition of salt to cheese has the following effects:

- Salt penetrates the curd, forcing more whey out.
- It initiates rind development by drying the surface of the cheese.
- Together with lactic acid, salt acts as a preservative
- Salt adds flavour.
- It inhibits the development of moulds, bacteria and yeasts.

Salt is applied in one of three ways:
- Addition of dry salt to the surface of the drained cheese.

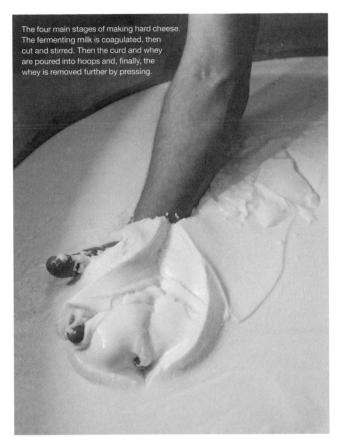
The four main stages of making hard cheese. The fermenting milk is coagulated, then cut and stirred. Then the curd and whey are poured into hoops and, finally, the whey is removed further by pressing.

Cheeses in a brine bath will float, so the exposed surface needs to be sprinkled with dry salt.

Same cheese - Crottin - made two days apart.

- Immersing the drained cheese in a saturated brine solution.
- Adding dry salt directly into the curds prior to the curds being placed in the hoop. (This is largely only done to cheddar or similar cheeses.)

The length of time a cheese spends in a brine bath, or the amount of dry salt that is applied to its surface depends on the type and size of the cheese. The final salt concentration is usually between 1.5–2.5% of the finished cheese. The salt may take several days or even weeks (in large cheeses) to become evenly distributed throughout the cheese.

## Maturation

This is the stage when different cheese varieties acquire their own typical texture, aroma and flavour through the complex physical and chemical changes that are unique to each cheese variety. To me, maturation is the real art of cheesemaking, but at a scientific level, maturation is mostly just bacteriological development, where enzymes are released that result in the casein breaking down into simpler protein forms. It is these enzymes that produce the specific aromas and flavours in cheese. Maturation takes place under specific conditions that are ideal for each cheese type. These conditions are a combination of temperature, humidity and time, as well as physical treatments such as washing and turning.

Industrial, mass-produced cheeses have limited maturation: hard cheeses are mostly vacuum-packed, preventing both rind development (which takes time and effort) and moisture loss (which equates to weight loss); and soft cheeses have a compromised maturation that employs special bacteria and enzymes to stop development and maximise the shelf-life of the cheese.

Rind development is a critical factor in the maturation of real cheeses. In hard cheeses, the presence of a good rind controls the progression of moisture from the inside out and, therefore, regulates the evaporation of moisture and the escape of gasses during maturation.

Hard cheeses are very slow to ripen and rely on the bacteriological changes within the cheese for maturation.

In soft, surface-ripened cheeses, such as white-mould or washed-rind cheeses, correct maturation conditions will encourage a good rind that supports the growth of desirable bacteria or moulds which release enzymes that break down the cheese from the surface towards the centre. This process should occur evenly and comparatively quickly. Cheeses will grow a surface flora of *Penicillin*. Washed-rind cheeses usually have a surface culture of *Brevi* bacteria.

In blue-mould cheeses, young cheese will often be punctured with needles to allow oxygen to get inside and activate the growth of aerobic blue-mould spores.

## MAKING CHEESE AT HOME

### It's easier than you think

Making delicious, safe cheese at home is totally achievable with a bit of care and knowledge. Maturation can be a bit tricky, though. Generally, the harder the cheese, the harder it will be to make at home. Fresh cheeses, such as fromage blanc (see page 111) and feta (see page 118), that do not require any maturation are as easy as pie to make. Start there, learn the techniques, understand how milk behaves and then start to branch out and try your hand at more complex cheeses.

### Before we get started, a word about hygiene

Rather than me telling you every time something needs to be clean, lets agree that everything that comes into contact with the milk, curd, whey or cheese needs to be free from bacteria. This also means you. Wash your hands. Lots. Having a really clean environment to make and mature your cheese is really, really important to achieve a good result. You can sterilise your equipment chemically using products like ammonia (stroll down your supermarket chemical aisle and there will be a frightening range of options) but generally this is unnecessary overkill for the home cheesemaker. Equipment that is washed in hot soapy water and allowed to air-dry is equipment that is clean. If you like, you can use boiling water to sterilise your tools (it's good to have a stockpot of boiling water on the go to keep your utensils in).

### You are going to need some milk

Not every house has a cow these days. In fact, it's highly probable that you don't even know anyone with a cow. So, what to do about milk? The best milk is always fresh (less than 24 hours old), unpasteurised and from a known source. But, if you can't source milk straight from your own animals or from a local farmer (look online for local dairies or dairy associations; depending on the regulations where you live you may be able to buy fresh, raw milk straight from the farmer), then you are going to have to buy bottled milk. Look for a brand that is unpasteurised (if you can find it), unhomogenised and from a single farm. If it has been pasteurised (which most bottled milk has) there is no need to pasteurise it again at home – it will still be fine to use, but the final product won't be as refined.

### Bacteria and rennet

You have some choices to make here. You can go down the natural cheesemaking route and allow the indigenous microflora in the milk to do the fermentation. Or you can purchase a commercial bacterial starter (see pages 280). In many of the recipes in this book, I suggest the use of 'live' yoghurt – that is yoghurt that has been pot-set using live bacteria (read the label and try to avoid products that have been thickened or sweetened).

For rennet, you can use plain junket tablets if you can find them in your supermarket (don't use the strawberry flavoured ones!), but it is worth purchasing a small bottle of rennet from a cheesemaking supplier, if possible.

### Cheese hoops

These are the perforated containers that you drain the curd in. The size and shape of the hoop will mould the curd and dictate the final form of your cheese. They are readily available from cheesemaking suppliers or you can fashion your own by poking lots of holes through a plastic container.

### What about a cheese cave?

Sadly, home cellars are even less common than house cows. That means if you are planning on making cheeses that require a bit (or a lot) of maturation, you will need to create a space that is clean, has a consistent low temperature, high humidity and a little bit of airflow. I have seen people successfully convert old fridges, polystyrene boxes, plastic tubs and eskys (coolers) into good cheese caves. You will just need to think about what will work for you in your own home. The ideal temperature range is 9°C–13°C (48°F–55°F) with about 80% relative humidity (you should see a little bit of condensation on the inside walls of whatever you use). To achieve airflow, try using a rectangular plastic container with a lid that has a few holes poked in it. Sit the cheese on a wire rack to keep it dry and to allow a rind to form all the way round.

Throughout maturation you will need to tend to your cheese regularly. Keep a close eye on it to notice any changes – this will help you establish if the cheese is too wet/dry or too cold/warm.

# HOW TO MAKE FROMAGE BLANC

This is just about the easiest cheese you can make at home, but it will still be way better than anything you can buy. That's because fresh cheese like this should be made and eaten within a day or two. Fromage blanc is the purest expression of fresh cheese and can be made with any good quality, fresh milk. Choose a milk that is unhomogenised and ideally one that comes from a single farm. If you are going to make this regularly, or if you want to experiment a bit, it's worth investing in some cheese cultures (see page 280).

MAKES ABOUT 1 KG (2 LB 3 OZ)
1.5 litres (51 fl oz/6 cups)
   full-cream (whole) milk
250 g (9 oz/1 cup) plain
   'live' yoghurt
1 dose of rennet (see note)

In a heavy-based stockpot over low heat, warm the milk and yoghurt, stirring constantly, to 35 °C (95 °F), using a sugar thermometer to assist you. Remove the pot from the heat and place in a bowl of water (or use your sink) also at 35 °C (95 °F) to maintain a constant temperature.

In a small stainless-steel bowl, dissolve the rennet in 100 ml (3½ fl oz) cool water. Add to the warm milk mixture and stir constantly for 3 minutes. Use a slotted spoon to stop the milk from moving (you need it completely still while the rennet is working). Place a lid on the pot and leave undisturbed for 1 hour.

Check to make sure the curd has set firm (it should come away easily from the side of the pot and you should be able to gently press your fingers on the cheese without it breaking).

Using a sharp knife, cut the curd into 5 cm (2 in) cubes. This will help the whey to escape from the cut surfaces. Let the curds sit undisturbed for 15 minutes. Using a slotted spoon or ladle, very gently lift the curds into a colander lined with a few layers of muslin (cheesecloth). Fold the excess cloth over the top and cover with plastic wrap. Place the colander in a bowl to catch the drips and transfer to the fridge to drain.

The fromage blanc can be eaten, unsalted, after 1 hour of draining but it will be firmer after about 8 hours.

After draining, transfer the fromage blanc to a bowl, season with salt and stir well. Store in an airtight container in the fridge for up to a week.

> **NOTE** Rennet comes in different strengths, so follow the packet instructions to see how much to use per 1 litre (34 fl oz/4 cups) of milk.

# FRESH CHEESES

Fresh cheeses are often overlooked in preference for those with more developed characteristics. What a shame! Fresh cheese can be an extremely sublime experience. From a delicate fromage blanc drizzled with honey, to the smack of feta crumbled over grilled vegetables, or the deep satisfaction of melted buffalo mozzarella on a pizza.

Fresh cheeses have no maturation. They are the purest and simplest expression of cheese and rely inherently on the quality of the milk for their exquisite flavour. The milk is fermented, often with the addition of starter cultures, which initiates lactic coagulation. This allows the natural and introduced lactic acid-producing bacteria to develop the acidity which gives these cheeses their lemony tang. They are drained to varying degrees, but require a fair bit of the moisture to be retained. Depending on the cheese, salt is sometimes added, assisting in the keeping qualities. They can be marinated in oil, pickled in brine, sprinkled in ash or left stark naked like the day they were born!

One special group of fresh cheeses is the 'pasta filata' cheeses, or stretched curd cheeses of Italy that include mozzarella, burrata and fior di latte. Stretching involves melting the drained, acidified curd with boiling water until in forms a molten mass. The cheese is then repeatedly stretched and pulled to align the proteins so that they form ribbons, which can be pulled around and sealed in on themselves to trap in moisture.

Because of their very high moisture content and often low salt content, fresh cheeses degrade very quickly. This means that they are best enjoyed in their region of origin and eaten within a few days of being made. Fresh cheeses travel poorly, except for the very commercial varieties, which are often low in moisture, highly salted and vacuum packed. Whenever I travel abroad, I make a point of eating these cheeses wherever I find them, knowing that they are not going to be seen outside of their home region.

## BENCHMARK FRESH CHEESES

### Feta (PDO since 2002)

Feta is like the crocodile of the cheese world, largely unchanged since its origins. It has been made in Greece for over 5000 years, making it the oldest cheese still available today. Traditionally, feta is always a mix of sheep's and goat's milk and it hails from a time when nomads tended herds on the dry mountains of central Greece. This tradition continued up until the mid-1900s when the nomadic people settled in towns and villages.

The sheep graze on the native herbs and grasses on the rocky slopes, where they are still tended to by shepherds today. The resulting milk is highly aromatic – perfect for this fresh cheese. Throughout Greece, feta is made using the same methods, but the milk will always give subtle regional variations. The holy grail is feta that has been aged in wooden barrels. I can still remember my first experience of it, given to me by my friend and fellow cheese-freak, Will Studd. Barrel-aged feta is made the same way as regular feta, which is packed in tins or plastic buckets, but instead of the normal strong brine used to store and ripen the

cheese, barrel-aged feta is packed in dry sea salt and covered with whey. The wood, and the microflora that lives in its grain, contribute a complex flavour that you will not find in regular feta.

Today, all feta needs to be made from pasteurised milk by law.

### Mozzarella di Bufala Campana DOC (PDO since 1996)

There are few joys in the cheese world greater than the experience of eating a fresh, still-warm ball of buffalo mozzarella in the hills of the Campana region behind Naples. Buffalo were introduced to the area centuries ago to work the marshy farmland, and the porcelain-white balls of fresh cheese made from their milk became a staple food of the region and an essential ingredient of pizza. Hand-made Mozzarella di Bufala Campana is the real thing (although buffalo mozzarella is now made in other parts of the country and around the world) and is characterised by a Y-shaped seal where the cheesemaker has pulled a layer of molten curd over the formed ball and sealed it between their thumbs and forefingers in an almost cutting motion. Inside, the ball should show layers of fragrant curd, dripping with creamy, lemony moisture that runs down your arm as you bite into it. This is not a strongly flavoured cheese and it is a great vehicle for other flavours – the classic combination being ripe tomatoes, aromatic fresh basil and pungent olive oil.

# HOW TO MAKE RICOTTA AND PANEER

Have you ever tasted fresh hot ricotta, straight from the pot? No? Well, you are in for a real treat! Making ricotta at home is a cinch, but the catch is that true ricotta should be made from whey, which means you first need to make some cheese to get the whey. Making ricotta from whey means that the milk has already gone through a fermentation process, which gives the ricotta a better taste and a lighter texture.

Ricotta made from whole milk is actually paneer. It isn't strictly a cheese as it hasn't gone through a fermentation process, but is instead curdled milk which has been strained and hung. To curdle the milk, you need a combination of high heat and acid. Lemon juice will work well but cheap, nasty white vinegar works best. Paneer is used all over India, especially in vegetarian cooking, and it makes a great substitute to meat in curries.

**MAKES 500 G (1 LB 2 OZ)**
5 litres (5¼ quarts) full-cream (whole) milk or whey
1 tablespoon salt
150 ml (5 fl oz) white vinegar

In a heavy-based stockpot over low heat, warm the milk (or whey if you are making ricotta) to about 60°C (140°F), using a sugar thermometer to assist you. Stir regularly to prevent the milk from burning on the bottom.

Stir through the salt then continue to heat the milk until it gets to 92°C (198°F). Do not let it boil or you will not be able to continue.

Dilute the vinegar with 200 ml (7 fl oz) water (this is so you get a good quick coverage). Remove the milk from the heat and immediately stir in the vinegar. Allow to rest for a minute, during which time you will see the curds rise to the top. Using a slotted spoon, lift the curds into a colander lined with rinsed muslin (cheesecloth) and place the colander in a bowl to catch the drips.

If you are making ricotta, set aside to cool for 5 minutes before using. If you are making paneer, bring the corners of the muslin together and tie into a bag. Hang this over your sink or a bucket and leave to drain overnight before using. Ricotta and paneer will keep, stored in an airtight container, in the fridge for 2–3 days.

---

### WHEY CHEESE

Traditional ricotta is made only from whey, which means that the protein has gone through a fermentation and is light and easily digestible. Commercial ricotta will often have milk or milk powder added in order to boost the milk solids and therefore the yield. The worst examples are made from just milk, which makes them feel heavy and cloying. Warm, freshly made ricotta is one of life's simple pleasures, but ricotta can also be aged, smoked or salted and dried.

You need to generate pretty big quantities of whey to make it worthwhile processing into cheese. Italy, Greece and Corsica have the strongest tradition of whey cheeses as whey is produced there as a by-product of making hard cheese.

# HOW TO MAKE FETA

Now we are getting serious. No more of the simple stuff, let's get into some real cheesemaking! Feta is such a versatile cheese and it's pretty simple to make. The best part is that it will keep for a few weeks, even though it doesn't require any maturation. Ideally, it is best made with fresh goat's milk, but if that's not possible you can still get good results with unhomogenised bottled cow's milk.

MAKES 500 G (I LB 2 OZ)

5 litres (5¼ quarts) full-cream (whole) milk
1 tablespoon plain 'live' yoghurt
dose of rennet (see note)
5 tablespoons sea salt

In a heavy-based stockpot over low heat, warm the milk to 32 °C (90 °F), using a sugar thermometer to assist you. Stir regularly to prevent the milk from sticking to the bottom.

Remove from the heat and sit the pot in a large bowl of water (or use your sink) heated to 37 °C (99 °F) to stop the milk from cooling. Stir the yoghurt through the milk and leave for 60 minutes, stirring occasionally.

Dilute the rennet in 250 ml (8½ fl oz/1 cup) water. Pour the mixture into the milk and stir for at least 3 minutes. Use a slotted spoon to stop the milk from moving (you need it completely still while the rennet is working).

Place a lid on the pot and let the milk mixture sit overnight at room temperature for 8–12 hours. Do not disturb it during this time.

The next day, the milk should have set firmly and should come away easily from the side of the stockpot. Use a sharp knife to cut the curd into approximately 1 cm (½ in) cubes. Very carefully, slice the curd vertically in one direction, then again at right angles. The hard bit is the horizontal cut to make the cubes. Use a clean hand and a gentle raking motion to move the curd from the bottom to the top to be able to cut it. Keep cutting until all the curds are roughly the same size (see illustrations on page 162 for reference).

Allow the curds to sit and 'rest'. After 10 minutes gently stir the cubes to stop them from knitting back together. Stir every 5 minutes for the next 30 minutes.

Line a colander with muslin (cheesecloth) and set over a bowl to catch the drips. Drain the curds from the whey by gently pouring through the muslin. Retain the whey and chill.

Find a plate big enough to cover the curds in the colander. You want the plate to sit on top of the curds and act as a weight. Place the plate on top of the curds and leave overnight at room temperature to press out any remaining whey. Remove the plate and turn the curds over a couple of times to help them drain evenly.

Add the salt to the chilled whey and stir until dissolved.

Cut the drained cheese into large cubes and place in a sterilised wide-mouthed jar with a tightly fitting lid. Cover with the salted whey.

Set aside in the fridge and let the feta 'pickle' for a couple of days before eating. Rinse off any excess salt before use.

The feta will keep, in an airtight container, in the fridge for 2–3 weeks.

**NOTE** Rennet comes in different strengths, so follow the packet instructions to see how much to use per 1 litre (34 fl oz/4 cups) of milk.

Barrel-aged feta is ripened in dry salt and whey.

# ARANCINI

Arancini are the party pies of Sicily. Resembling little oranges, from which they take their name, outside of Sicily they are seen as a good way of repurposing last night's leftover risotto. But that is doing them an injustice, as risotto is from the north of Italy and almost never cooked as a dish in the south, where traditionally arancini are made from scratch. I prefer eating arancini warm, but cold is equally fine.

I have used bocconcini as the filling in this recipe, which gives the arancini a soft cheesy centre, but you can use any filling you like. You can make your arancini using 370 g (13 oz/2 cups) leftover risotto, just bring it to room temperature first.

**MAKES ABOUT 10**

800 ml (27 fl oz) chicken stock
250 g (9 oz) arborio rice
big pinch of saffron, steeped in 1 tablespoon hot water for 2 hours
100 g (3½ oz) parmesan, grated
100 g (3½ oz) provolone, or any other semi-hard cheese, chopped into chunks
10 bocconcini
1 egg
50 g (1¾ oz) plain (all-purpose) flour
300 g (10½ oz) dried breadcrumbs
vegetable oil for deep-frying

If starting from scratch, this is the way the Sicilians prepare the rice – it's quite different from making a risotto. Bring the stock to the boil in a medium-sized saucepan, then add the rice and saffron water. Bring back to the boil, then reduce the heat right down to a low simmer and cook, without stirring, until the stock is absorbed and the rice is cooked through. Remove from the heat and stir in the grated parmesan and the provolone. Season with salt and pepper. Spread the rice out on a baking tray, cover with plastic wrap and set aside to cool completely.

To make the arancini, wet your hands and take a small handful of rice. Roll it around in your hands to form a shape that's bigger than a golf ball, but smaller than a tennis ball. Poke a hole in the middle with your finger, insert a bocconcini then squish the rice around to cover the hole. Set each ball aside while you keep going until all the rice is used up.

Make a batter by beating together the egg, flour and enough water to give it a thinnish consistency. Put the breadcrumbs on a plate.

Heat the oil in a deep saucepan to 180°C (350°F), or until a grain of rice dropped in sizzles as soon as it hits the oil. Dip each rice ball in the batter to coat, then roll in the breadcrumbs until completely covered. Shake off any excess crumbs, then fry the arancini in batches of 3–4 at a time, so that the oil does not cool down too much. Turn them over regularly to ensure that they cook evenly. When the arancini are golden brown, remove from the oil and drain on paper towel. Sprinkle with salt and serve hot.

120

## PDO AND PGI CHEESES

In 1992, European lawmakers created two systems to protect traditional and regional foods. Protected Designation of Origin (PDO) dictates that the cheese must be traditionally and entirely manufactured within a specific region. To receive Protected Geographical Indication (PGI) status, the cheese must be traditionally made and at least partially manufactured within a specific region to maintain its unique properties. These systems replaced the French certification of Appellation d'Origine Controlee (AOC) and the Italian certification of Denominazione di Origine Controllata (DOCG).

Stretched curd cheeses can either be fresh, like mozzarella, or aged, like provolone (centre) and cacio cavallo (above).

# MOZZARELLA IN CARROZZA

Anywhere in the world where there is bread and cheese there is a version of the grilled cheese sandwich. The French have the croque monsieur, the British have the Welsh rarebit, the Aussies have the jaffle and in Italy, there is mozzarella in carozza. Dead simple and delicious. Keep it simple and enjoy its purity or use it to carry other flavours such as basil, anchovies or tomato.

MAKES 2
4 thick slices white bread
1 ball buffalo mozzarella
olive oil for shallow frying
125 ml (4 fl oz/½ cup) full-
   cream (whole) milk
1 egg, beaten
3 tablespoons plain
   (all-purpose) flour

Remove the bread crusts and discard. Cut the mozzarella into slices about 4 mm (¼ in) thick. Arrange the slices on two pieces of bread and sandwich together with the remaining slices of bread. Squish the edges of the sandwich together to help seal the bread.

Pour the milk into a shallow bowl and the beaten egg into another bowl. Season the egg with salt and pepper. Finally, put the flour on a plate.

Heat the oil in a large, heavy-based frying pan over medium heat.

Working from left to right, dip the sandwiches in the milk, then coat both sides lightly in flour before dunking in the beaten egg. Fry both sides until they are golden and crisp and the cheese is melted. Serve immediately.

124

# RICOTTA GNUDI WITH BUTTERY PEAS

This recipe will make it look like you have spent the day cooking but really, you could pretty much make it in the ad breaks of your favourite soap opera. I have used mushy, buttery peas to accompany the gnudi, but ricotta is such a great vehicle for other flavours that you could use just about any pasta sauce.

SERVES 4

100 g (3½ oz) salted butter
12 sage leaves
500 g (1 lb 2 oz) frozen peas
2 tablespoons pure cream (35% fat)
1 tablespoon lemon juice

GNUDI

350 g (12½ oz) fresh ricotta
25 g (1 oz) grated hard cheese, such as parmesan or similar grana-style cheese
1 egg yolk
¼ teaspoon freshly grated nutmeg
225 g (8 oz) fine semolina, plus extra for dusting

To make the gnudi, mix the ricotta, grated cheese, egg yolk and nutmeg in a medium-sized bowl. Tip the semolina into a shallow baking dish and dust a plate with a little extra semolina. Working quickly with damp hands, roll a tablespoon of the ricotta mixture in your hands to form a rough ball. Roll it in the semolina and then form into a smooth ball, about the size of a golf ball. Place on the plate and continue until all of the ricotta mixture is used – you should end up with about 12 dumplings. Cover the gnudi with plastic wrap and place in the fridge for an hour to firm up.

Melt the butter with the sage leaves in a heavy-based frying pan over medium heat. Remove from the heat just as the butter is starting to brown.

Bring a large saucepan of salted water to the boil and add the frozen peas. Simmer for five minutes until tender. Remove the peas with a slotted spoon and transfer to a food processor with the cream and lemon juice. Process until almost smooth. Add to the melted butter and stir to combine. Pour into a serving dish and set aside.

Bring the water to the boil again, then reduce to a simmer. Working in two or three batches, add the gnudi and cook for about 3 minutes, or until they float to the top. Remove with a slotted spoon, drain well and serve on top of the warmed buttery peas.

# ROAST BEETROOT AND FETA TART

This tart is all about the feta. You could easily swap out the roast beetroot for roast pumpkin, leeks or any other veggies you like.

SERVES 6

2 large beetroot (beets), peeled and each cut into 8 wedges
olive oil, for drizzling
4 eggs
1 egg yolk
1 French shallot, peeled and finely chopped
400 g (14 oz) crème fraîche
2 tablespoons chopped flat-leaf parsley
200 g (7 oz) feta, crumbled

SHORTCRUST PASTRY

340 g (12 oz) plain (all-purpose) flour, plus extra for dusting
150 g (5½ oz) chilled butter, chopped
2–3 tablespoons iced water

Preheat the oven to 190°C (375°F).

To make the shortcrust pastry, put the flour and butter in a food processor and pulse until the mixture resembles breadcrumbs. Gradually add the water, a little at a time, until the mixture starts to come together. Turn out onto a clean work surface and form the dough into a ball. Wrap in plastic wrap and refrigerate for 30 minutes.

Put the beetroot in a baking dish and drizzle over a little olive oil. Season with salt and pepper, and roast for 30–40 minutes, or until cooked through.

Lightly grease a 25 cm (10 in) round loose-bottomed tart tin, about 3 cm (1¼ in) deep.

On a lightly floured work surface, roll the pastry out to a 3–4 mm (¼ in) thick circle. Transfer the pastry to the tart tin – it should be large enough to line the base and side of the tin, with enough excess pastry to hang over the edge. Place on a baking tray and chill for 30 minutes.

Line the tart base with baking paper and add some baking weights. Blind bake for 20 minutes, then remove the weights and baking paper and continue cooking for a further 5 minutes, or until the base is golden. While the pastry is still warm, trim the edge of any excess pastry. Reduce the oven temperature to 160°C (320°F).

Whisk together the eggs, egg yolk, shallot and crème fraîche in a bowl. Season with salt and freshly ground black pepper, then fold in the parsley and half of the cheese. Pour the mixture into the tart base, making sure the feta is evenly distributed. Bake for 20 minutes, then carefully remove from the oven (the tart will be wobbly and only half cooked at this stage). Top with the roast beetroot and the remaining feta. Return to the oven for a further 20 minutes, or until set. Serve warm or cool.

# CURED OCEAN TROUT, GRAPEFRUIT AND GOAT'S CURD

This is a great combination of colours, flavours and textures.

SERVES 8 AS A STARTER
1 kg (2 lb 3 oz) ocean trout
    fillet (or Atlantic salmon)
200 g (7 oz) raw sugar
200 g (7 oz) salt
1 large beetroot (beet), grated
30 g (1 oz/½ cup) dill,
    chopped, plus extra
    to garnish
zest of 1 lemon
1 grapefruit
150 g (5½ oz) fresh goat's
    cheese
100 g (3½ oz) salmon roe
extra-virgin olive oil, for
    drizzling

Lay the fish fillet skin side down on a chopping board. Run you fingers along the length of it, feeling for bones and removing any with fish tweezers.

Combine the sugar, salt, beetroot, dill and lemon zest in a bowl. Lay the fish in a shallow baking dish and cover both sides with the sugar and salt mixture. Cover with plastic wrap and place in the fridge for 4–8 hours to cure.

Rinse the curing mixture from the fish and pat dry. Using a very sharp filleting knife, cut the fish into very thin slices – cutting almost parallel with the chopping board – but do not slice through the skin. Set the slices of cured fish to one side and discard the skin.

With a small, sharp knife, slice away the peel and pith of the grapefruit, exposing the flesh. Use your knife to cut out the flesh in between the segments. Set these to one side.

On a serving platter, randomly arrange the slices of ocean trout. Add the grapefruit segments along with pieces of the goat's cheese, followed by the salmon roe. Garnish with a few sprigs of dill, finish with a drizzle of olive oil and serve.

130

## WHAT'S THE STORY WITH RAW MILK CHEESES?

The subject of raw milk and raw milk cheese has been a hot topic for as long as I have been making cheese. There are some very strong opinions (and often not a lot of facts) on both sides of the debate. It is symbolic of the divide that exists in many areas of our food production, namely the chasm of disconnect that often lies between the producer, the scientists and the consumers.

I have seen otherwise intelligent people nearly come to blows over this issue, then make peace over a pint of pasteurised beer. So why does the issue of raw versus pasteurised milk cheese get people's backs up so much?

Possibly it is the tradition. But more than that, I think this debate goes to the core of the discontent much of society feels when our food gets manipulated. We feel like our autonomy is being threatened, our ability to live the life we choose, make our own decisions and be guided by our own common sense. We tolerate this in almost every aspect of our lives, but when it happens to our food, we seem to take it more as a personal attack.

### Pasteurisation

Pasteurisation of milk is an excellent thing … when it is needed. For well over a century it has prevented diseases including tuberculosis, brucellosis, diphtheria, scarlet fever, and Q fever and has made milk a globally important source of food.

Pasteurisation was first employed in 1862 by, as the name suggests, Louis Pasteur as a way of preventing wine and beer from souring. It was not until 1886 that the same technique was applied to milk, making it also safer to drink. This was important because after the industrial revolution the world became rapidly urbanised. The time it took to get milk from the country to the city was getting longer and the milk would often spoil before being consumed.

Pre-industrialisation, this was not such an issue because, even in urban areas, house cows were extremely common.

Pasteurisation is the name given to the heat treatment of milk (and other liquid foods such as juice, eggs and beer) to destroy pathogenic bacteria, which can cause illness. Pasteurisation does not sterilise the milk but it does destroy most of the good bacteria as well as all of the bad. The process temperature can vary and it is always in combination with a minimum time. The typical standard in the dairy industry is to process at 72°C (162°F) for 15 seconds.

Pasteurisation (and refrigeration) is the reason milk now has a use-by date some 2–3 weeks after it has left the farm. In contrast, UHT milk has been heated to a minimum of 138°C (280°F) for 2 seconds. This destroys all the bacteria in the milk, which is why it does not need to be refrigerated and has a ridiculous shelf life. It also denatures the proteins and caramelises the natural sugar in the milk, which is why it tastes so awful. Even when kept at less than 2°C (36°F) raw milk will start to deteriorate – it has a lifespan of 4–8 days because of the naturally occurring bacteria.

There are many arguments for and against raw milk cheese. Here are the three main ones:

### Food Safety

Because pasteurisation kills bacteria, it is the first and foremost reason countries in the West have mandatory pasteurisation laws for all commercial dairy products. It is a safety net designed to protect the lowest common denominator. However, these laws are becoming less defensible because unsafe cheese can still be made using pasteurised milk. Raw milk cheese can be made safely. It happens every day, in dozens of countries by thousands of cheesemakers. The risks in making raw milk cheese

132

Bruny Island Cheese Company's raw milk C2.

are identical to those when making pasteurised milk cheese and it is what we, as cheesemakers, do that determines the safety of our cheeses. Properly produced, raw milk does not kill people. If we start with fresh, clean milk from healthy animals raised in good conditions, and process it into cheese using sound practices that respect some basic principals of microbiology, then safe cheese will always be the result.

Raw milk from healthy animals is, fundamentally, a safe food. It is a complete food source for newborn mammals, rich in protein, vitamins, minerals, hormones and bacteria. In fact, it is close to being a perfect growth medium for these vital bacteria. But it is also the perfect growth medium for pathogenic bacteria.

Cheese is a fermented food. Fermentation is a natural and ancient food preservation technique which can render unsafe foods safe. The primary fermentation in cheese is the conversion of lactose (the sugar in milk) into lactic acid. This job is done by bacteria, which occur naturally in milk.

Cheesemaking is basically the process of acidification (fermentation) of milk and the removal of water. This acidification is crucial in producing a safe cheese. It is important because through fermentation, these good bacteria will decrease the pH of the milk, producing an unfavourable environment for the growth of pathogenic bacteria. Also, the proliferation of the good bacteria will produce an environment which is strongly competitive, making it difficult for colonies of the pathogenic bacteria to establish in harmful numbers. This is especially the case for raw milk.

In cheesemaking, post-pasteurisation contamination is a real risk. This is because pasteurisation removes much of the good bacteria as well as all the bad. The good bacteria form a natural defence in the milk, and if this defence mechanism is removed or compromised, then undesirable bacteria can become established and flourish quickly. This is why rapid acidification of

pasteurised milk is an essential step in cheesemaking. In Europe, many cheeses are made with 'pre-ripened milk'. Pre-ripening is the process of adding a small amount of lactic acid-producing bacteria to the milk stored at a warm temperature (usually 10°C–20°C/50°F–68°F) for up to 12 hours before it is made into cheese. This is done to proliferate the good bacteria. It also develops better flavours in the milk and cheese. In Europe, for many cheeses it is a legal requirement to do this. The milk for Comté (the biggest selling cheese in France), for example, is legally not allowed to drop below 10°C (50°F). This practice is unfortunately largely illegal in Australia, the UK and the USA. Still, there are those who maintain that pasteurisation is essential to producing safe cheese. There are also those (including some very highly regarded scientists) who see pasteurisation as a threat to food safety.

We were making cheese long before we had food scientists, and we are playing catch-up a bit. For the past 50 years or so we have taken a very conservative, risk-averse approach to food production – one that has shunned centuries of traditional food production and relied wholly on the point of view of science. This has resulted in many of our traditional foods being compromised or lost. Today there is a better understanding of the time-proven methods that have long produced food that is safe and pleasurable, so that science can now inform our food production, alongside tradition, rather than dictate to it.

## Flavour

Fans of raw milk cheese maintain that pasteurisation destroys the natural flora in the milk which deliver so much of the character and flavour of the cheese. This is true but it is not an absolute truth.

Raw milk cheese does have more character than the same cheese made on the same day from the same milk, only pasteurised. This is a taste test I have done several times, with several different cheeses in several different locations. The results have always been clearly in favour (and flavour) of the raw milk version.

But that does not mean that all raw milk cheese has superior flavour to pasteurised milk cheese. I have tried some bloody revolting raw milk cheese in my time (I've even made a few of them). Likewise, I have also tasted plenty of pasteurised milk cheeses that have made me swoon (I'd like to think that I was responsible for a few of those, too).

In the 90s I worked at Neal's Yard Dairy in London – a veritable library rich with UK artisan and farmhouse cheeses, staffed by some of the most cheese-obsessed individuals on the planet. On any given day the slate tasting bench groaned under the weight of around 100 different cheeses, sourced from every nook and cranny of Britain and Ireland. All but five were unpasteurised. At lunch, the staff had free access to the full range and it never ceased to amaze me that these cheese freaks who spent their days espousing the flavour benefits of raw milk cheese, routinely selected Colston Basset Stilton, by law made with pasteurised milk, for their own sustenance. The reason was simple: it tasted utterly incredible.

The other problem in relying on flavour as an argument is that it is not on the radar of the food regulators, and neither should it be. Their job is to regulate the production of food so that the risk to public safety is minimised. Like organic produce, raw milk can deliver great flavour in cheese, but it is not a sure thing.

### Terroir and integrity

Terroir is the essence of the place where a cheese is made. It is what gives a cheese its unique, regional character. Terroir is influenced by everything that makes a place unique. It is an expression of a cheesemaker's integrity and unfortunately, pasteurisation is the enemy of this integrity. As a cheesemaker, I want to be able to use my skills to make the best cheese possible. Being made to use pasteurised milk does not allow me to do this. The rich flora found in raw milk is determined by several factors: the breed, age and health of the animal, the soil, the climate, the pasture, the supplementary feed such as hay or silage, the quality of the air and water the animal consumes, to list just a few of the big ones. Combined, these produce a milk which is true and unique to that specific animal and farm. Pasteurisation removes much of that special character.

In Europe, this is taken very seriously. Protected Appellations of Origin (PDO) is a system to ensure that these characters are not compromised or lost (see page 122). In the Australian wine industry, we now place a high value on the terroir of wines. It is what sets two wines of the same variety, vintage and region apart. Yet in Australia, it is a conundrum to me that we do not value terroir in cheese. In fact, we are legally obliged to stamp it out through pasteurisation. Yet, artisan and farmhouse cheesemakers in countries like Australia rely on this point of differentiation from more commercially produced cheeses which are becoming more and more competitive on quality and price but who are not in a position to make raw milk cheese. These regulations must be changed, not only to recognise that raw milk cheese can be made safely but also to allow for the development of real cheese with true regional character.

135

# THE DEFINITIVE MARGHERITA PIZZA

It's important to know how to make pizza at home. And I am not just talking about adding a few ingredients to a commercial pizza base. Unless you live in the south of Italy, home-made pizza is better than bought pizza 99.9% of the time. There are two tricks to great pizza: the first is self-control – use only a few top quality ingredients and use them sparingly. The 'less is more' mentality is a very difficult thing for most humans to master, especially kids. But, if we can learn this simple approach to life we could fix everything from climate change to bad pizza! The second trick is using the right cheese, and the correct cheese for margherita is fresh buffalo mozzarella.

I like my bases a bit puffy. If you are the same, the trick is not to drown the base in tomato sauce and don't spread the sauce to the edge of the base. This also gives you something to hold onto without getting your fingers messy. Oh, yeah, that's another thing … only use your hands to eat pizza!

**MAKES 6 PIZZAS**

3 balls fresh buffalo
    mozzarella, cut into 5 mm
    (¼ in) thick slices

**PIZZA BASE**

400 ml (13½ fl oz) warm
    water
2 tablespoons active dry
    baker's yeast
1 teaspoon raw sugar
700 g (1 lb 9 oz) plain (all-
    purpose) flour, plus extra
    for kneading and dusting
½ teaspoon salt
2 tablespoons olive oil
semolina, for sprinkling

**PIZZA SAUCE**

400 g (14 oz) tinned crushed
    tomatoes
2 garlic cloves, finely
    chopped
2 tablespoons olive oil
¼ teaspoon sugar
2 tablespoons basil leaves,
    plus extra for topping

To make the pizza base, mix the water, yeast and sugar in a small bowl using a fork. Set aside – after 10–15 minutes it will start to look foamy on top. Place the flour and salt in a large mixing bowl and give it a quick whisk (that's my cheat's way of sifting). Add the yeast mixture and the olive oil and mix with a wooden spoon until it all comes together. Turn out onto a lightly floured work surface and knead the dough with your hands for 15 minutes or until the dough is smooth and elastic. Place in a lightly oiled bowl, cover with plastic wrap and set aside somewhere warm for 30 minutes to rise.

To make the pizza sauce, place the tomatoes, garlic, olive oil, sugar and basil leaves in a saucepan and bring to the boil over medium heat. Reduce the heat and simmer for 30 minutes to reduce the sauce by about one quarter. Remove from the heat and let it cool a little. Season with salt and pepper.

Preheat the oven to 240°C (460°F) – really crank it up! Tip the dough back onto a floured work surface and divide into six equal-sized balls. Working with one ball at a time, roll out to a circle large enough to fit your pizza tray or pizza stone (unless of course you are lucky enough to have your own wood-fired pizza oven – then bake directly on the hearth). The dough should be about 5 mm (¼ in) thick. Lightly oil the pizza tray and sprinkle with semolina to stop the dough from sticking. Lift the base onto the tray and use you fingers to stretch it into the right size and shape. If you have multiple pizza trays, loosely cover each base with plastic wrap and set aside before moving on to the next.

Spread a small amount of tomato sauce on each base with the back of a spoon – remember the 'less is more' philosophy! Arrange 4 or 5 slices of the mozzarella on top and sprinkle over a few basil leaves.

Bake each pizza for 10–12 minutes and serve straightaway.

136

# HONEY, WHISKY AND SAFFRON CHEESECAKE

Oddly, I first made this onboard a boat that me and my mates Matthew Evans and Ross O'Meara were sailing around Tasmania, filming *Gourmet Farmer*. Making dessert on the boat seemed like a special occasion because normally, by the end of a day's sailing, we were exhausted and a toasted sandwich, a chunk of chocolate and a nip of whisky was all we could manage before we flopped onto our bunks (except that my bed doubled as the dinner table, so I had to wait until the boys were finished). This is my favourite Tasmanian recipe.

SERVES 8

500 g (1 lb 2 oz) mascarpone

a few saffron strands, steeped in 1 tablespoon boiling water for at least 1 hour

160 g (5½ oz) caster (superfine) sugar

1 tablespoon leatherwood honey, warmed

4 eggs

50 ml (1¾ fl oz) whisky

SWEET SHORTCRUST PASTRY

190 g (6½ oz) plain (all-purpose) flour

90 g (3 oz) cold unsalted butter, cut into 1 cm (½ in) cubes

1 tablespoon caster (superfine) sugar

1 egg yolk

2 tablespoons cold water

To make the pastry, rub the flour, butter and sugar between your fingertips until it resembles breadcrumbs. Alternatively you can use a food processor to do this. Add the egg yolk and water, and mix until the dough comes together to form a ball. Wrap the dough in plastic wrap and set aside in the fridge for at least 30 minutes to rest.

Mix the mascarpone, saffron water, sugar, honey, eggs and whisky together in a large bowl. Set aside.

On a lightly floured work surface, roll out the pastry to about 4 mm (¼ in) thick. Line a well greased 23 cm (9 in) springform tin with baking paper and carefully place the pastry in the tin. Trim the edge of any excess pastry and return to the fridge to chill.

Preheat the oven to 180°C (350°F).

Line the pastry base with baking paper and weights, and blind bake for 15 minutes. Remove the weights and baking paper and bake the tart shell for a further 10 minutes.

Pour the filling into the tart shell and bake for a further 30 minutes, or until set and golden on top. Allow to cool before serving.

# ROSS'S RICOTTA SHORTCAKE

My mate Ross O'Meara is not known for his delicate nature, or his desserts. But this subtly delicious tart was one of the first things he ever cooked for me when he landed on Bruny Island. Sweet, warm ricotta wrapped in a crumbly, short pastry … This is a really beautiful way to use up fresh ricotta.

SERVES 6

icing (confectioners') sugar, for dusting

ground cinnamon, for dusting

SWEET SHORTCRUST PASTRY

300 g (10½ oz/2 cups) plain (all-purpose) flour, plus extra for dusting

50 g (1¾ oz) caster (superfine) sugar

3 tablespoons icing (confectioners') sugar, plus extra for dusting

1 tablespoon baking powder

½ teaspoon salt

125 g (4½ oz) chilled butter, diced

2 eggs

FILLING

650 g (1 lb 7 oz) fresh ricotta

3 egg yolks

3 tablespoons icing (confectioners') sugar, sifted

finely grated zest of 2 lemons

To make the pastry, place the flour, caster sugar, icing sugar, baking powder, salt and butter in a food processor and pulse until the ingredients are well combined and resemble breadcrumbs. Add the eggs one at a time and keep pulsing until the mixture forms a ball. Turn the dough out onto a lightly floured work surface and knead gently. Separate one third of the dough and wrap the two balls separately in plastic wrap. Chill in the fridge for at least 1 hour.

To make the filling, combine all of the ingredients in a bowl and set aside.

Preheat the oven to 180°C (350°F).

Lightly grease and line a 23 cm (9 in) springform tin. Roll out the larger dough ball on a work surface lined with baking paper and form a circle large enough to cover the base and side of the tart tin. The pastry should be at least 5 mm (¼ in) thick. Work quickly because as the pastry warms up, it will become quite fragile. Carefully line the base and side of the tin with the pastry. Patch up any holes or tears with spare bits of pastry and trim any excess pastry overhanging the edge of the tin, leaving a few millimetres (¼ in) exposed above the tin.

Gently scrape the ricotta mixture onto the pastry base and use a spoon to spread it evenly and to the edge. Roll out the remaining pastry to a circle big enough to cover the tart. Lay it over the filling and then pinch the base and the top together to seal. Trim the edge so that it is neat.

Cook in the oven for 20–30 minutes until the pastry is golden. Allow to cool for 30 minutes in the tin before removing. Serve at room temperature, dusted with icing sugar and cinnamon.

140

## NATURAL CHEESEMAKING

Natural cheese is made without the addition of starter cultures, using only the indigenous bacteria in the milk for the fermentation process. Milk will definitely start to ferment naturally given the right conditions, namely warmth and time, because it is full of lactic acid bacteria. I love this notion as it really appeals to the innate traditionalist in me. This is undoubtedly the way cheese was made in the past, and there are still some big-name examples of cheeses around the world where this approach is used. But... and there are a couple of big 'buts' for me, the complete lack of control that goes with natural cheesemaking means that steering the curd toward a predetermined outcome becomes much harder, especially if you are wanting to make consistent, regular batches. This is because milk, and the bacteria found in it, constantly changes depending on all sorts of variables.

Also, relying on the natural bacteria in milk to do your work comes with the real risk of allowing any bad bacteria that may be present in the milk (those that can spoil your cheese or even cause food poisoning) to also get established.

Cheeses such as Salers and Cantal in France or Ragusano in Italy (all respected cheeses made commercially and exported around the world) are all made using a form of natural cheesemaking. But it is important to understand that their success and consistency comes from the fact that they are made in environments that are literally saturated with the desired bacteria through years of making the same cheese, every day and taking steps to manage those colonies. Maturation rooms (including mine) are full of indigenous moulds and bacteria as well, providing cheese with their own specific terroir.

The key to successful natural cheesemaking at home is firstly the quality of your milk. You really need to know where it is from and how it has been produced to understand how it may transform into cheese.

Goat's and sheep's milk have a naturally lower bacterial count than cow's milk, so maybe head in that direction. You also need to be OK with the 'let's just see what grows' approach. The results can be anywhere from vile to stunning, but they will always be interesting. Using a commercial starter bacteria for the fermentation is definitely not a bad thing – it will give you a great and consistent result – but if you want to dabble in the natural world a bit, then go for it, let the native microflora take control of your cheese.

# WHEY POPS

Joe Graff, one of my cheesemakers on Bruny Island, makes these and sells them at local markets. Joe uses whey as a base instead of cream and milk, which makes them terrifically refreshing. This recipe is for his roasted plum version but you could use the same method for any other kind of fruit.

MAKES 6
45 red cherry plums
3 tablespoons raw organic
  sugar

WHEY SYRUP
500 ml (17 fl oz/2 cups) fresh
  whey
75 g (2¾ oz/⅓ cup) raw
  organic sugar
2 tablespoons loose-leaf
  black tea

Preheat the oven to 200°C (400°F).

To roast the plums, place them in a baking tin and sprinkle the sugar over the top. Roast for 25 minutes or until the plums are tender and their juices have been released.

Pour the plums, juice and all, into a fine-meshed sieve over a medium-sized bowl. Mash the roasted plums through the sieve so that all the fruit transfers into the bowl leaving the pits and skins behind.

To make the syrup, pour the fresh whey into a small saucepan over medium heat. Add the sugar and tea leaves, stir and let simmer for 10 minutes. Remove the whey syrup from the heat and pour through a fine-meshed sieve into a medium-sized bowl. Set aside to cool a little. Discard the tea leaves.

Add the whey syrup to the roasted plums, stir to combine and divide between six ice-pop moulds. Insert wooden ice-cream sticks into the base of each mould and freeze overnight.

144

---

### WHEY

You know when you take a spoonful of yoghurt out of a jar and come back the next day to find a pale yellow puddle in the yoghurt? That's whey. Whey is the bacterially rich liquid that remains once you have made cheese and removed the curds. But left behind in the whey are very small amounts of milk solids. These can be recovered by heating the whey and adding acid – which is exactly how ricotta is made (see page 116).

At home, you can use whey in place of water in cooking. In his epic book *The Art of Fermentation*, Sandor Katz describes several uses for whey as a starter culture. It also adds a lovely, soft acidity to salad dressings.

# WHEY HOT TODDY

Whey makes a delicious drink. It is sweet and acidic and can be drunk straight up or flavoured. Historically, in Northern Europe, whey was fermented to become alcoholic and served in cafés and inns – they still drink it as a cold sparkling drink in Sweden and Iceland.

On cold days, at my cheesery on Bruny Island, we will take a jug of fresh whey, sweeten it with local honey and froth it under the steam wand of the coffee machine. It's even better with a bit of whisky in it!

SERVES 2

400 ml (13½ fl oz) fresh whey
60 ml (2 fl oz/¼ cup) whisky
1 tablespoon honey
1 tablespoon lemon juice
1 cinnamon stick
lemon peel, to garnish
   (optional)

If you have a coffee machine with a steam wand, place all the ingredients in a jug and use the wand to heat and slightly froth the whey. Alternatively, heat the ingredients in a small saucepan until warmed through (although you won't achieve a frothy head).

Serve, garnished with slices of lemon peel (if desired).

# WHEY AND SOURED CREAM BREAD

When you begin to make a bit of cheese at home on a regular basis you will also start to produce a fair amount of whey. Substituting whey for water in bread is not only a great way to use it up but also produces a bread with a slightly sour taste and a denser crumb. It's kind of a cheat's sourdough in this respect. This is a great sandwich loaf.

MAKES 1 LOAF

2 teaspoons active dry yeast
1 teaspoon caster (superfine) sugar
250 ml (8½ fl oz/1 cup) whey, warmed
125 g (4 oz/½ cup) crème fraîche
550 g (1 lb 3 oz) bread flour, plus extra for kneading and shaping
2 teaspoons salt

Activate the yeast by mixing it with the sugar and a little of the whey in a small bowl. Leave to stand for 10 minutes until it becomes a bit frothy.

Whisk the crème fraîche and remaining whey in a large mixing bowl. Add the flour, salt and yeast mixture and mix with a wooden spoon until it forms a rough ball. Cover and let sit for 10 minutes.

Turn the dough out onto a lightly oiled work surface and give it a light knead for 1 minute. Cover with plastic wrap and let the dough rest on the benchtop for 5 minutes. Knead for 2 minutes then rest for another 5 minutes. Knead for 3 minutes, then place in a lightly oiled bowl, cover with plastic wrap and leave to rise in a warm place for 1 hour.

Lightly oil a loaf (bar) tin. Tip the dough onto the work surface and use your palms to flatten it out. Roll it up and place in the loaf tin, with the seam on the bottom. Cover with plastic wrap and place in a warm spot for a further 1 hour.

Preheat the oven to 190°C (375°F).

Bake the dough for 40–50 minutes, until it has risen and is golden on top. Allow to cool completely before slicing.

148

# LE SAPALET DAIRY

I visited Le Sapalet in the middle of winter. Not the ideal time from a cheesemaking point of view but it was unforgettably picturesque with snow-covered mountain peaks providing the backdrop for deep white valleys and tiny towns. It's not the easiest farm to find. The drive winds through the mountains and the beautiful surrounds make it hard to concentrate on the road.

This is still very much a family affair with Jean-Robert's brother, daughter and three of his nephews all involved. One of his nephews, Joakim Henchoz, is in charge of making the cheese while another runs the business and another tends to the flock.

In summer, the sheep (and about 30 goats) graze the mountain pastures, accompanied by a pair of large, white Maremma dogs that guard the flock. The only access to the flock is by foot and the shepherding is carried out the same way it has been for centuries. Although sheep seem out of place here – this is very much cow country – they also seem perfectly suited to the steep slopes and natural herbage. When winter comes, the flock is walked down the mountain and housed in a large barn where they are given a rest and kept warm, dry and well fed.

Le Sapalet is a small organic farm on the edge of a village called Rossinière in the Pays-d'Enhaut region of Switzerland. It was started by Jean-Robert Henchoz who previously milked cows and made L'Etivaz cheese in the mountains above where the current dairy stands. In the 1990s Jean-Robert's wife Anne got enthusiastic about sheep and started milking a flock of 11 Lacaune ewes. By 2000, that flock had grown to 180 and they sold their remaining 40 cows and concentrated on making sheep's milk cheese.

The family has recently built a new cheesemaking facility that allows Joakim to make a range of different cheeses as well as butter and yoghurt. I spoke to him about the benefits of working in a family-run operation.

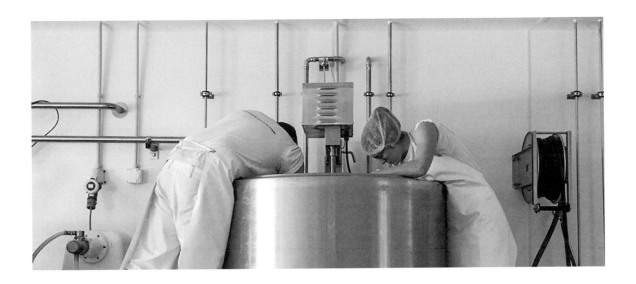

**MILKING SHEEP IS NOT TRADITIONAL IN THE SWISS ALPS. WHY DID YOU CHOOSE TO GO AGAINST TRADITION AND MAKE SHEEP'S MILK CHEESE?**

*Because my aunt Anne loved them and wanted their milk for her daughters, who couldn't digest cow's milk. A few years later, the herd became bigger and the milk has become better known and appreciated. Cow's milk also holds less value than sheep's milk, so my uncle and aunt decided to change. Et voilà!*

**THERE IS A HUGE SEASONAL VARIATION IN YOUR MILK BETWEEN SUMMER AND WINTER. HOW DOES THAT PLAY OUT IN YOUR CHEESE AND BUTTER?**

*There are more proteins and polyunsaturated fatty acids in summer grasses, so the resulting butter is softer. The milk is rich in omega 3 and 6 and subsequently makes better cheeses!*

**HOW DOES THE DIET OF THE SHEEP CHANGE THROUGHOUT THE YEAR?**

*In summer, we graze the sheep on mountain pastures, so they only eat very good grass. In winter and spring, they eat hay and silos of grass and maize.*

**YOURS IS A FAMILY OPERATION – YOUR BROTHER RUNS THE FARM, YOU MAKE THE CHEESE WITH YOUR COUSIN, YOUR OTHER BROTHER DOES THE SALES AND MARKETING. WHAT IS THE BEST AND WORST THING ABOUT BEING INVOLVED IN A FAMILY BUSINESS?**

*I think we only have the best! We are family AND friends so we're happy to work together. We're all 'pulling at the same rope'! We pay attention to each other and hold regular meetings so that everyone can express themselves and be heard. Family or not, it's always important that everyone has their own place.*

**IN YOUR MATURING ROOM YOU HAVE A ROBOT THAT TURNS AND RUBS YOUR HARD CHEESES. WHAT ARE THE BENEFITS OF THIS? DO YOU LOSE ANY QUALITY WHEN NOT TURNING AND RUBBING THE CHEESE BY HAND?**

*It saves us precious time and pain to have a robot do the hard work. But we always monitor the cheese, as it can be necessary to moisten them more than two times a day, depending on the atmosphere. We would never have time to do all this work.*

The next generation of the Henchoz family
at Le Sapalet in Rossinière, Switzerland.

# SURFACE-RIPENED CHEESES

Few families of cheeses are more loved or more recognisable than soft, oozy, rinded cheeses. Brie and camembert are synonymous with this category, replicated and imitated around the world, but they are only two members of this huge and varied family.

## MOULD-RIPENED CHEESES

The pure white rinds of these cheeses is a modern affectation and a result of single strains of mould being isolated and grown by people wearing lab-coats. Traditionally, cheeses in this family were exposed to the natural environment and consequently had rinds of multiple strains of white, grey or even blue mould.

Today, the strains of mould favoured by cheesemakers are *Penicillium camemberti* and *Penicillium candidum*. *Geotrichum* is another variety that is often associated with soft, surface-ripened goat's cheeses and is recognised by its ivory-coloured, wrinkly skin. The spores of these moulds are usually inoculated directly into the milk so that they immediately flourish once the maturation conditions are favourable. A new cheese, if matured around 12°C–15°C (54°F–59°F) in a high humidity, will start to display the first fuzz-like signs of exterior mould growth between 5–8 days.

These soft, surface-ripened cheeses develop from the outside in and break down over time until their centres are soft and unctuous. By cutting large curds and handling them very gently, the cheesemaker retains as much moisture as possible in order to produce the desired texture in the matured cheese. In the case of camembert, the curd is scooped with a ladle rather than cut and drained, and in the best examples this is done by hand. After the cheeses have drained overnight in their hoops, they are salted either with dry salt on their exterior or by immersing in brine for a short time before being moved to maturation rooms. Spotting the difference between mass-produced mould-rinded cheeses and the real stuff is not too hard. Use all of your senses to evaluate each cheese. The best examples will have rinds with an obvious variety of moulds and bacteria at work. They will not be perfectly white, and may have mottled patches as they develop (we need to wean ourselves off the 'perfect red apple' mentality). A cut cheese may have a chalky centre if it is on the young side, or it might be uniformly oozy if fully developed. Ask your cheesemonger if you can give it a gentle squeeze. To touch, it will be firmer in the centre than on the edges, showing that it is maturing traditionally. In these cheeses, it is the rind that is doing the maturation, so the older the cheese, the more mature and developed the rind will be. It should smell clean, funky, earthy and farmy. Ammonia is produced by mould in its later stages of life and is generally an indication that the cheese is in its latter stages of maturation. These are not simple cheeses – they are tricky to make and mature and their window of perfection is short. Some of you will prefer them on the younger side, when they are full of vigor and vibrancy; others will like the stronger, deeper, richer versions as they head towards being fully ripened. Take the time to choose and you will be rewarded.

In more commercial varieties, where the thick, carpet-like rind of pure, white mould is largely an affectation that has little effect on the development of the cheese, special starter cultures are used to regulate their maturation to provide stability and longer shelf life. Great for supermarkets, terrible for the cheese-loving consumer. This also makes them perfect for selling as pre-cut wedges (which should be avoided).

## BENCHMARK MOULD-RIPENED CHEESES

### Camembert de Normandie AOC
### (PDO since 1996)

Camembert is made everywhere, right? No! The genuine article, Camembert de Normandie AOC, comes only from Normandy in northwest France. Anything else is, at best, a fake and, at worst, an insult.

The creation of Camembert de Normandie is credited to a woman named Marie Harel, who fortuitously gave refuge to a priest from Meaux (home of Brie) who shared with her his knowledge of cheesemaking. Proximity to Paris helped to secure the reputation of the cheese from the village of Camembert.

Truly great artisan versions of this cheese are hard to find, even in Normandy; despite the rigorous controls applied to its manufacture, most of the ten-or-so producers who make Camembert de Normandie are industrial in their size and approach. Unfortunately, the name camembert is not protected (which is why cheese under this name is made all over the world) and the regulations controlling the manufacture of Camembert de Normandie still allow for the cheese to be made on a massive scale. Sadly, the vast majority of it is now made by robotic manufacturing lines.

But when you get a great example, this cheese is just about as good as it gets. Richly pungent, deliciously unctuous and extremely generous on the palate, it is no wonder this cheese has become a benchmark of quality since the 1700s.

### Brie de Meaux AOC (PDO since 1996)

Despite being one of the oldest and most iconic of all French cheeses, and one that is copied widely throughout the world, the production of real Brie is actually in decline and there are now just six artisan producers left. Because of its close proximity to Paris, the small region of Île-de-France, where the only real Brie is made, is becoming consumed by urban sprawl and Mickey Mouse (it is also the site of Euro Disney).

There are actually several different varieties of Brie made in the Île-de-France. All are unique and with different qualities, but all have in common their ability to make you go weak at the knees with their heady aroma of wild mushrooms and delicious, sticky buttery interiors.

Brie de Meaux is perhaps the most famous. By law it is only made from raw milk and formed into large, flat 3 kg (6 lb 10 oz) discs. Straw is also used in its traditional manufacture and maturation. Other varieties of Brie include Brie de Nangis, Brie de Melun (my favourite) and Brie de Coulommiers.

### Sainte-Maure de Touraine AOC (PDO since 2003)

The Loire Valley, in the central-west of France, is home to an array of wonderful soft, mould-rinded goat's cheeses. Truth be known, it is hard to single out just a couple of noteworthy benchmarks. Apart from this one and the Cabécou de Rocamadour (discussed below), seek out other AOC examples such as Selles-sur-Cher, Chabichou du Poitou, Pouligny-Saint-Pierre and Crottin de Chavignol to further your education in the seductive world of mould-rinded cheeses.

Sainte-Maure de Touraine should not be confused with the cheese called Sainte-Maure, which is the industrial version and whose manufacture is a series of cheesemaking compromises. The real deal, however, is a study in dedication to quality. Made only seasonally when the goats are in full lactation, this long, log-shaped cheese has a piece of straw inserted through the middle to give it strength (I am also convinced the microflora on the straw contribute a unique character). The curds undergo lactic coagulation over 24 hours and the rind is dusted in powdered charcoal, through which grey-white moulds and *Geotrichum* become established over the 2–4 week affinage. It is truly one of the world's benchmark goat's cheeses.

### Cabécou de Rocamadour AOC (PDO since 2008)

This is a tiny cheese whose character belies its size. Because it is so small, it has a shelf-life of usually less than two weeks and is rarely of much quality outside of the region of Lot, but when you find a good example in its homeland, it is a lesson in how good cheese can be. The rind is typically formed from *Geotrichum*, a supple, bloomy skin that holds back an ivory-coloured explosion of wonderfully goaty flavour.

## WASHED-RIND CHEESES

No group of cheeses gets my blood up more than the soft, pungent, stinky and utterly delicious washed rinds. Their ephemeral earthiness is deeply satisfying, especially when matched with a well-considered beverage. Like their mould-rinded cousins, washed-rind cheeses develop from the outside in. But unlike those mouldy, bloomy cheeses, for these little funksters it's all about bacteria.

*Brevibacterium linens* is the bug of choice. *Brevi* (for short) is an endemic bacteria that grows in damp places and is also commonly found on human skin. Washing the rind (usually in a brine solution) not only provides a moist environment for *Brevi* to thrive but the action of washing helps transfer the microflora from cheese to cheese and batch to batch. As a result, washed-rind cheeses are all generally moist or sticky to the touch and have a characteristic pinky-orange coloured rind. They are also stinky, or as a posh lady at a tasting once described to me, they are 'a little bit close to the cow's tail'.

These are tough cheeses to make because of the attention required to develop their rind to perfection, and as a result they are also victims of modern, industrialised techniques that stabilise the curd and fake the rinds by washing them in food colouring. These industrialised cheeses usually have a very consistent texture throughout and are mild and boring compared to the real thing.

Traditional washed-rind cheeses are highly aromatic. The smell can instantly transport me to a farm. Many people are offended by this smell, which is a great shame because what lies beneath are some of the most intense and sensual experiences in the cheese world.

## BENCHMARK WASHED-RIND CHEESES

### Époisses de Bourgogne AOC (PDO since 1996)

This odiferous cheese has allegedly been banned from being taken onto public transport in Paris. Made from cow's milk sourced from Simmenthal and Montbéliarde breeds in the hills north-west of Dijon, it is now mostly made by larger producers from pasteurised milk.

Developed by Cistercian monks in the 15th century, Époisses is possibly the quintessential washed-rind cheese. The wrinkly red/orange rind is so beyond sticky it is almost slimy, as a result of the frequent washing in brine over its 4–5 week maturation and then with Marc de Bourgogne (a local spirit) for its final treatment, which creates an aroma that can clear a room. Époisses is right up there with the other great washed-rind cheeses of France, along with Pont-l'Évêque, Livarot and Maroilles.

### Taleggio (PDO since 1996)

From a country that makes some of the best hard cheeses in the world, Taleggio stands alone as one of the few Italian washed-rind cheeses. My friend and mentor, Will Studd, gave me a masterclass on Taleggio in 1998 when he took me to see the cave-ripened versions in the steep mountains west of Lake Como. These cold, damp caves housed fat, square forms of Taleggio in hundreds of wooden trays. The cheese develops slowly because of the low temperature.

Unfortunately, even in Italy, most Taleggio is mass-produced rubbish, which is waxed or vacuum-packed and aged in cool rooms. The good stuff is only made in the region of Lombardy, has a pale pink-orange rind and a soft, buttery texture.

Washed-rind cheeses at Consider Bardwell Farm in Putney, Vermont, USA.

159

# HOW TO MAKE WHITE-MOULD CHEESE

Making a soft, surface-ripened white-mould cheese at home is easier than you think. Like most cheese, the maturation is where you can come unstuck, so it is worth taking the time to set yourself up with a place to mature your cheese (see page 163).

HERE IS WHAT YOU
WILL NEED:

8 litres (2.1 gallons) fresh unhomogenised full-cream (whole) milk

¼ teaspoon commercial bacterial starter culture or 1 tablespoon 'live' yoghurt

thermometer

10 litre (2.6 gallon) stainless-steel stockpot/double boiler (or equivalent)

slotted serving spoon

syringe to measure the rennet

2–3 ml (¼ fl oz) rennet

long-bladed serrated knife (a bread knife is fine)

20 litre (5.3 gallon) plastic box with lid (this will be your cheese cave)

8 cheese hoops about 10 cm (4 in) diameter

wire rack to fit inside plastic box

salt

**Preparing the starter (the day before)**

In a small saucepan boil, then cool, 200 ml (7 fl oz) of the milk. Transfer the milk to a sterilised, dry glass jar with a tight fitting lid. Add ¼ teaspoon of commercial starter culture or 1 tablespoon of 'live' yoghurt and stir well. Screw the lid on and store the jar at 25°C–30°C (77°F–86°F) until the mixture thickens to the consistency of yoghurt (approximately 12–24 hours). If this does not happen, you will need to start again with some fresh starter. Your starter will store in the fridge for a couple of days until needed.

**Preparing the milk**

If you are going to pasteurise the milk, follow the instructions on page 104, then cool it back down to 33°C (91°F). If you are using fresh, raw milk, place it in your stockpot and place over a low heat until it reaches 33°C (91°F). Alternatively, heat the milk over a water bath. Stir regularly with your slotted spoon to make sure the milk doesn't burn or catch on the bottom.

Remove the pot from the heat and place in a bowl of water (or use your sink) heated to 35°C (95°F). You want to keep the temperature of the milk between 32°C–35°C (90°F–95°F). Adjust the temperature of the water bath to warm or cool your milk as required.

**Add the starter culture**

Add the prepared starter culture and mix well through the milk. Cover your stockpot and set aside for 75 minutes.

**Renneting**

Use the syringe to measure out the rennet in a small bowl. Dilute the rennet with 50 ml (1¾ fl oz) water. Gently stir into the milk with an up and down motion for at least 1 minute. Once you are satisfied that the rennet is completely stirred through evenly, you need to use your slotted spoon to stop the milk from moving around in your stockpot. Cover the stockpot again and leave to set for 60 minutes or until you get a 'clean break' (see below).

**Testing for a clean break**

Slide your finger into the curd at a 45 degree angle and lift it up towards the surface. If the curd breaks cleanly around your finger and whey runs into the crack left behind, you have a 'clean break'. The curd is ready to be cut. If it still seems a bit sloppy and did not form a clean break, give it another 10 minutes.

### Cutting the curd

Use the illustrations at right as a guide to cut the curd into 2 cm (¾ in) cubes. Leave to stand for 20 minutes to set.

### Stirring the curds

Using extremely clean hands or your slotted spoon, turn all the curds over gently for 3 minutes – try and bring the curds on the bottom up to the top. It will be very fragile at this stage so go easy. Any larger curds that come up from the bottom may be cut at this stage. Do this another 3 times, 5 minutes apart. Note how much whey is released over time as the curds get firmer. Taste the curd at this point – it should be sweet and clean tasting.

### Preparing the curd

After the final stir, let the curds rest and sink into the whey. Using a glass or ladle, scoop out about 60% of the whey and discard (or keep it to make ricotta, see page 116). After the whey has been removed, give the curds a gentle stir to stop them from knitting back together. You are trying to keep all the curds separate from each other.

### Filling the hoops

Making sure that your cheese cave, wire rack and hoops have been sterilised (I sit everything in boiling water), set up your cave with the wire rack sitting on the bottom of the box with your hoops on top.

Using your slotted spoon, scoop a small amount of curds into each hoop, then go back and put more in each and so on until they are evenly filled. Fill the hoops just short of the top. If the curds look enormous, don't worry, when turned repeatedly they will settle down to the thickness required. Leave to drain for 20 minutes.

### Turning the hoops

The reason you turn the cheese is to give it a good shape and also to drain it evenly. This can be a bit tricky at first. Basically, you need to slide the cheeses out of their hoops, turn upside down and slide them back in. The trick is to do this with the hoop on its side rather than upright. That way you can cradle the cheese in your hand and slide it back into the hoop before inverting it. If you make a mess of it, don't worry too much; the curds should fix themselves more or less.

You will need to do this every 30–60 minutes for 5 turns in total. Place the lid on the box between turns to keep any dirt out. If the bottom of the box fills up with whey, discard it, as you do not want the cheese sitting in whey. Leave the cheeses overnight.

162

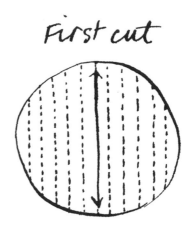

First cut

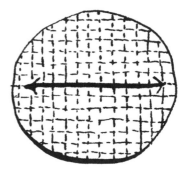

Second cut

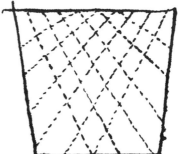

Horizontal cut

## Salting the cheese

The following morning the young cheese will have firmed up and should pull away easily from the edges of the hoops. This indicates that the cheese can now be removed for salting.

Take the cheeses out of the hoops and lightly sprinkle a little salt over the top of each cheese. Leave to stand for 15–30 minutes. Turn the cheeses over and lightly sprinkle the bottom and sides with more salt and let stand for a further 15–30 minutes. You only want to use 1–2 teaspoons salt per cheese.

Shake off any excess salt and place the cheeses back on the wire rack in the box. Place the lid back on and keep the box somewhere around 15°C (60°F) overnight.

## Ageing the cheese

This is the tricky bit. For the next 7–14 days you need to find a place to store the cheese cave that is (a) between 10°C–14°C (50°F–57°F), (b) clean and out of reach of pets, pests and children and (c) easily accessible. Turn your cheese daily (literally, turn it over) and discard any moisture that collects in the bottom of the box. After 5–7 days you should notice a light fuzz of white mould on the rind. This is a good thing. The cheese should be totally covered with white mould after 10 days.

## Monitor the cheese daily

The only other problem at this stage is humidity – or generally, a lack of it. If the cheese feels dry to the touch, add some wet kitchen towel to help boost the humidity. If there is excessive condensation on the lid of the box, this can drip onto the cheese causing a yellowish slime. If this happens, remove the lid, wipe away the moisture and replace the lid leaving it slightly ajar.

## Wrapping the cheese

Once the cheeses are fully covered in white mould, they are ready to wrap. Use a material that will allow the cheese to breath, such as waxed paper. Don't use plastic wrap or foil. Centre each cheese on a square of paper and fold the corners onto the cheese until it is completely covered. Place the wrapped cheese back into the box with the folded side on the bottom. Put the lid back on and age for a further 2–4 weeks at 11°C–15°C (52°F–59°F).

## When is it ready to eat?

The perfect cheese should be soft and creamy and bulge slightly when it is cut. You may want to experiment with ageing times and temperatures to achieve the texture and flavours you prefer.

SOCIÉTÉ
DE LA

FROMAGÈRE
BRIE

36/30

36/36

PRODUIT _Vignelait_

DATE DE FABRICATION  _19 01 09_

QUANTITÉ

LOT

DATES DE RET

Brie de Meaux in various stages of production
and maturation in Île de France, France.

## WHAT'S THE DIFFERENCE BETWEEN BRIE AND CAMEMBERT?

This is certainly not a question that you would ever hear in France. But it is an important question as it typifies the divide between traditional cheesemaking countries such as France and the New World. I have visited some pretty big-name makers of cheese in Australia who make both 'brie' and 'camembert' and, hand on my heart, the only difference between the two is the roll of labels on the packaging line. This is why I feel so passionate about cheesemakers creating cheeses that speak of the place they are made, rather than copying cheeses made on the other side of the world in a complete absence of the assets which make those cheeses unique.

Yes, the two cheeses are similar in-so-far as they are both soft, white-mould cow's milk cheeses but that is where the similarities end. Brie comes from the Île-de-France, a small, inland region near Paris. Camembert comes from the maritime region of Normandy on the northwest coast of France. The soil, climate, native pasture and climate are quite different in both locations. Their size also sets them apart: brie is a 35 cm (14 in) wide disc weighing in at 3 kg (6 lbs 10 oz), whereas camembert is only 11 cm (4½ in) across and weighs about 250 g (9 oz). The size has a profound effect on how the cheese matures. Camembert curd is ladled into the hoops, whereas brie has its curd cut and poured into the hoops. Different breeds of cow, different qualities in the milk, different bacteria, I could go on … There are literally dozens of differences that separate these two cheeses. Just ask a French person.

# BAKED ONIONS IN BRIE CUSTARD

This is great as a stand-alone vegetarian dish or as a fancy side dish to roast chicken. I have used brie in this recipe, but you could use any mould-ripened cheese that has a bit of flavour. You could even use a funky washed rind if you like.

SERVES 2 AS A MAIN COURSE
OR 6 AS A SIDE DISH
8 small red onions
4 eggs
4 egg yolks
200 ml (7 fl oz) thick
    (double/heavy) cream
200 ml (7 fl oz) full-cream
    (whole) milk
150 g (5½ oz) brie, or similar
    soft cheese, rind removed,
    cut into cubes
6 thyme sprigs, leaves picked
boiling water

Preheat the oven to 200°C (400°F).

Trim both ends of the onions and peel, but leave whole. Place on a baking tray, season and bake in the oven for 40–50 minutes until cooked through and golden brown on the outside. Set aside to cool. Reduce the oven temperature to 160°C (320°F).

In a large bowl, whisk the eggs and egg yolks very thoroughly – there should be no egg white visible. Set aside.

Place the cream and milk in a saucepan over low–medium heat and bring to a low simmer. Immediately add the brie and stir until completely melted and incorporated into the milk and cream. Remove from the heat, season with salt and pepper and allow to cool for a few minutes.

Slowly pour the milk mixture into the beaten egg, using a whisk to gently stir as you go (don't add too much air).

Arrange the onions in a 2 litre (68 fl oz/8 cups) capacity ceramic baking dish or ovenproof saucepan. Carefully pour the custard mixture around the onions and sprinkle over the thyme. Place the dish in a deep baking tin and pour enough boiling water into the tin to come halfway up the sides of the dish. Bake until the custard sets completely, about 30 minutes. Allow to cool slightly before serving.

166

# CHEESY POLENTA WITH MEATBALLS

This is a roll-your-sleeves-up, all-in-together kind of dish. The creamy and cheesy polenta is the star. I don't bother with individual plates – just pour the polenta on a big board or plate, top with the meatballs and let everyone dig in.

## SERVES 6
2 tablespoons olive oil
600 ml (20½ fl oz) tomato
  pasta sauce (bought is fine)
½ teaspoon chilli flakes
1 tablespoon oregano leaves
2 fresh bay leaves
freshly grated parmesan,
  to serve

## MEATBALLS
1 small onion, chopped
2 garlic cloves
4 slices pancetta
handful of flat-leaf parsley
  leaves
6 sage leaves
3 slices white bread, crusts
  removed
300 g (10½ oz) minced
  (ground) pork
300 g (10½ oz) minced
  (ground) lean beef
2 eggs

## POLENTA
500 ml (17 fl oz/2 cups)
  chicken stock
500 ml (17 fl oz/2 cups) full-
  cream (whole) milk
300 g (10½ oz) instant polenta
  (fine cornmeal)
100 g (3½ oz) fontina cheese,
  rind removed, cut into
  small cubes (see note)
1 rosemary sprig, leaves
  picked

Start with the meatballs. Put the onion, garlic, pancetta, parsley, sage and bread in a food processor and pulse until finely chopped. Add the pork and beef mince and eggs, and keep pulsing until well combined. Season well with salt and pepper. Transfer to a bowl and finish mixing by hand. Using wet hands, form the mixture into walnut-sized balls, setting them aside on a plate as you go.

Heat the olive oil in a heavy-based saucepan over medium heat. Carefully add the meatballs and cook until they start to brown on all sides. Add the tomato sauce, chilli flakes, oregano and bay leaves and simmer for 30–40 minutes until the meatballs are cooked and the sauce is reduced and thick.

To make the polenta (this will take 10–15 minutes, so try and time it to be ready at the same time as the meatballs), place the stock, milk and 500 ml (17 fl oz/2 cups) water in a large saucepan and bring to the boil. Gradually add the polenta and use a whisk to stir it through until well incorporated. Reduce the heat to low and stir continuously for 3–4 minutes until the polenta is thick and creamy in texture. Add the cheese and rosemary and stir until the cheese is melted through.

To serve, pour the polenta onto a large serving platter and make a shallow well in the middle. Spoon the meatballs and sauce over the top and sprinkle with some freshly grated parmesan. Serve immediately.

> **NOTE** Fontina is a mild washed-rind cheese from the Valle d'Aosta in the north of Italy and is one of the best melting cheeses I know. Raclette is a good substitute, or any other washed rind with the rind removed.

168

# TARTIFLETTE

This is mountain food. And by mountain, I don't mean the type that bearded hunters stalk across. Or the type of mountain that lonely climbers seek to conquer. It's the kind of mountain where you will find tartiflette dished up and served to skiers and snowboarders, for whom nothing short of melted cheese and potatoes will sate their hunger at the end of the day. I would love to tell you that tartiflette has been sustaining skiers and farmers in the French Alps for centuries, but I can't. It was concocted in the 1980s by the marketers of Reblochon in order to sell more of their cheese. Who cares. It tastes great. Cut the rind off the Reblochon if it is too strong, but make sure you still have 600 g (1 lb 5 oz) of cheese. Raclette or any mild washed-rind cheese are good substitutes.

SERVES 6

1.3 kg (2 lb 14 oz) waxy potatoes, unpeeled
4 tablespoons unsalted butter
250 g (9 oz) bacon, rind removed, cut into 3–4 mm (¼ in) thick strips
1 large onion, thinly sliced
170 ml (5½ fl oz/⅔ cup) dry white wine
200 ml (7 fl oz) whipping cream
1 garlic clove
600 g (1 lb 5 oz) Reblochon or similar washed-rind cheese, cut into 1 cm (½) thick slices

Boil the potatoes in plenty of salted water until almost cooked (bigger ones may take a little longer than smaller ones). Drain and set aside to cool down.

Preheat the oven to 190°C (375°F).

Melt 2 tablespoons of the butter in a heavy-based frying pan over medium heat. Add the bacon and onion and sauté until the onion starts to carmelise. Add the wine and stir with a wooden spoon to get all the tasty bits off the bottom of the pan. Bring to the boil and allow the mixture to reduce until almost all of the wine has evaporated. Remove from the heat and stir through the cream.

Cut the potatoes into bite-sized chunks. Fry them in the remaining butter in a large frying pan over medium heat, until golden.

Rub an ovenproof dish or pan with the garlic clove then cover the base with half of the potatoes. Spoon half of the cream mixture over the potatoes and then arrange half of the cheese slices on top. Repeat this process with the remaining half of the ingredients. Bake in the oven for 15 minutes then finish under the grill (broiler) to give it a bit of a crust.

Serve hot with a simple salad.

170

# FIG, BRIE AND ROSEMARY TART

Sweet, fattened figs. Pungent, oozing brie. I blush to think what these two perfect bedfellows could get up to behind closed doors. Like figs themselves, this tart is neither very sweet nor very savoury. It could be served as a light lunch with a green salad or as a dessert with sweetened yoghurt.

SERVES 6–8

200 g (7 oz) brie, rind removed

2 eggs, beaten

35 g (1¼ oz) caster (superfine) sugar

150 ml (5 fl oz) thick (doubly/heavy) cream

6–8 fresh figs, halved

8 small rosemary sprigs

PASTRY

110 g (4 oz) unsalted butter, softened

110 g (4 oz) caster (superfine) sugar

¼ teaspoon baking powder

240 g (8½ oz) plain (all-purpose) flour, plus extra for dusting

1 egg

To make the pastry, pulse the butter, sugar, baking powder and flour in a food processor until it resembles breadcrumbs. Add the egg and keep pulsing until the mixture forms a ball. Wrap the dough in plastic wrap and rest in the fridge for 1 hour.

Preheat the oven to 190°C (375°F).

On a lightly floured work surface, roll out the dough until it is 3–4 mm (¼ in) thick. Lay it over a 20 cm (8 in) tart ring set on a baking tray lined with baking paper. Patch-up any cracks or holes and trim the edge of any excess pastry. Line the tart base with baking paper and add some baking weights. Blind bake for 20 minutes then remove the baking weights and paper and continue cooking for a further 5 minutes. Set aside to cool.

In a medium-sized bowl, mash the brie well with a fork. Mix in the beaten egg, sugar and cream and stir until well combined.

Arrange the fig halves in the tart shell cut side up. Carefully pour the brie custard around the figs, stopping about 2 mm (⅛ in) from the top of the pastry. Sprinkle the rosemary sprigs on top. Bake for about 40 minutes or until the custard is set and the top golden. Allow to cool completely before serving.

172

# LINGUINE WITH MUSHROOMS AND STINKY CHEESE

Creamy, earthy, funky, stinky. Four of my favourite words, all in the same dish. What's not to love?

SERVES 4

400 g (14 oz) dried linguine
50 g (1¾ oz) unsalted butter
2 tablespoons extra-virgin olive oil
1 medium onion, finely chopped
500 g (1 lb 2 oz) mixed mushrooms, roughly chopped
100 ml (3½ fl oz) dry white wine
200 g (7 oz) crème fraîche
300 g (10½ oz) washed-rind cheese, rind removed, cut into small cubes
handful of flat-leaf parsley, chopped

Bring a large stockpot of salted water to the boil. Add the pasta and cook until al dente.

Meanwhile, heat the butter and oil in a heavy-based frying pan over high heat. Add the onion and sauté for 2 minutes. Add the mushrooms and cook for about 5 minutes, or until they are almost cooked through. Add the wine, bring to the boil and cook until the liquid has reduced by half. Add the crème fraîche and the cheese, bring to the boil again, then reduce the heat and simmer for 3 minutes, stirring occasionally.

Drain the pasta, return to the pot and toss through the mushroom mixture and parsley. Serve immediately.

174

# THE PINES DAIRY

In 1841, George Grey left Northern Ireland to start a new life in Australia. Landing in Sydney, he travelled south to the coastal settlement of Kiama and purchased land which included a homestead property known as 'The Pines'. George Grey established the property as a dairy farm and bred cattle that would later become the antecedents of the famed Illawarra Shorthorn breed. Six generations later, Kel Grey and his wife Cassandra and father Garry still operate a dairy farm.

Today, the farm is smaller and runs only a small herd of 17 Holstein cows with the milk bottled and sold to make gelato and yoghurt.

**THIS IS ONE OF THE SMALLEST COMMERCIAL DAIRY FARMS IN AUSTRALIA. HAS IT ALWAYS BEEN SUCH A SMALL HERD?**

*At its height, there was a herd of around 120 cows, which back then put the farm at the larger end of the scale. But the big difference between now and then is the production. When the farm was carrying 120 cows, milk output was only 8–10 litres (2.1–2.6 gallons) per day per cow. These days we get about 26 litres (6.9 gallons) from each cow, although when my dad was milking he was able to push them to about 34 litres (9 gallons) per day.*

**SO, WHAT HAS CHANGED TO GET SUCH A BIG DIFFERENCE IN MILK PRODUCTION?**

*Three things. Firstly, breeding has changed with the introduction of artificial intelligence, which has meant that farmers can now accelerate the quality of their herd. Secondly, feeding the cows supplements, such as hay and grain, has increased milk productivity, and lastly the implementation of strip grazing means the cows are getting more grass.*

Garry and Kel Grey.

### CAN YOU EXPLAIN YOUR STRIP GRAZING REGIME?

*The cows are put on new grass after their morning and afternoon milkings. We have 20–25 cows and our strips are about 1 acre (½ hectare) with a 30 day rotation. That means that each strip is grazed for one day and then rested for 30 days.*

### DO YOU FEED THE COWS SILAGE?

*No. I have heard lots of mixed reports about silage but the old Italian farmers I have spoken to say that the flavour and aroma of fermented feed goes through the milk. And besides, we have a great hay farm.*

### WHY DO YOU ONLY FARM HOLSTEINS?

*Dad lives to breed the perfect cow – and he loves Holsteins! For me, when I was growing up, my favourite cheese was cheddar – real farmhouse cheddar. So when I saw that cheddar came from the green hills of Somerset that were dotted with black and white cows, I decided that was what I wanted to do. Making a good hard cheese is still my ultimate goal. I also like the milk of Holsteins – it's finer textured and less heavy than other breeds.*

### TO GET MILK, A COW NEEDS TO HAVE A CALF. WHAT DO YOU DO WITH YOUR CALVES ONCE THE COW HAS GIVEN BIRTH?

*We raise all of our calves, the boys and the girls. Some of the bulls are kept for breeding stock. The rest are steered and hand raised for 6 months before joining our beef herd and raised until they are at least two years old.*

### WHEN I LOOK AT YOUR FARM AND YOUR FARM PRACTICES I SEE THINGS, BOTH ETHICALLY AND SUSTAINABLY, THAT ARE VASTLY DIFFERENT TO THE REST OF THE DAIRY INDUSTRY IN AUSTRALIA. THAT IS OBVIOUSLY A CHOICE, SO WHY HAVE YOU CHOSEN TO DO THINGS DIFFERENTLY?

*Ethically I could not live happily with some of the things that go on on conventional dairy farms. The problem as I see it is the system. Farms sell their milk to milk companies who are usually multi-national public companies that are driven by profit and shareholder return, so they drive down the price they are willing to pay for milk. This means that farms need to get bigger to gain efficiency through economies of scale, and also make decisions regarding the way they farm based on their own profitability over sustainability or ethics. Rather than questioning the validity and value of this system, farmers just keep trying to get what they can out of it by pushing their land and animals. In doing so we move further and further away from a natural and sustainable agricultural system.*

177

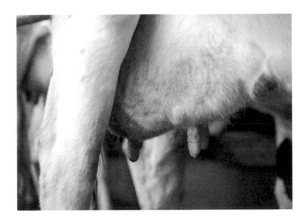

The odd girl out; this is the only Jersey among the Grey's herd of Holsteins. Kel reckons breeding the perfect Holstein is his dad Garry's reason for living.

# BLUE CHEESES

# Of all the families of cheese, blue-mould cheeses seem to divide even the most hardcore cheese freaks.

People often tell me that they don't like blue cheese – some even have a complete inability to entertain the notion of eating mould (yet these people will happily hoe into a camembert – go figure). I think what they really mean is that they don't like bad blue cheese – and there is plenty of this stuff made and exported around the world for people to try and form such an opinion.

Blue cheese is one of the oldest groups of cheese, having been made for millennia. They are characterised by the growth and distribution of blue-green mould inside the cheese. Mould, being aerobic, needs air to grow, so the distribution of this mould is often in the tiny air pockets that form between the curd particles. Blue cheeses are commonly pierced with needles to further facilitate the introduction of air into the cheese. Consequently, one of the most challenging of all cheese varieties to make is soft blue cheese, as the curd collapses as it breaks down, preventing any air from entering.

Many blue cheeses are rindless, but use a barrier layer such as foil to prevent them from drying out. Others have a wonderfully crusty rind that is developed over time through scraping and rubbing the exterior.

Modern production techniques and the use of highly specialised, laboratory-derived strains of blue mould have resulted in many new varieties of blue-mould cheese around the New World. For my money, rarely do they transport your senses like some of the traditional benchmarks in this field.

## BENCHMARK BLUE CHEESES

### Roquefort (PDO since 2008)

You can't have a conversation about blue cheese that does not include Roquefort. From the village of the same name on the Causse du Larzac in the centre of France, Roquefort has an extraordinary history and is held in the highest regard by cheesemongers around the world. The Roquefort-sur-Soulzon's Mont Combalou is home to a series of limestone caves that have long been the secret to the cheese's affinage.

Traditionally, Roquefort was made on farms where the raw milk from a local breed of sheep, Lacaune, was turned into cheese before being sold to cave owners to complete its maturation by storing it where the iconic *Penicillium roqueforti* blue mould would grow in cool, damp conditions. These days, despite production now lying entirely in the hands of just seven large producers (look for the names Carles or Yves Combes for the best examples), traditional production and maturation is still largely adhered to, including limiting the production season from December–July, and using bread to grow and propagate the mould spores. Despite some of the more cognoscente of the older generation feeling that the abandonment of farm production and the modern use of refrigeration and foil to complete the cheese's maturation has been to the detriment of its quality, the fact remains that few cheeses deliver such sensual pleasure as Roquefort.

### Stilton (PDO since 1996)

For the weeks leading up to Christmas in 1993, I had the job of tasting and grading every wheel of Stilton at London's iconic cheese shop, Neal's Yard Dairy, and selecting which wheels would be cut to sell that day. It was a fascinating experience and exposed me to the nuances of this cheese in a way that nothing else could.

The history of this quintessential English blue cheese dates back to the early 1700s where it was first made commercially by a lady named Frances Pawlett from Leicestershire. Farmhouse Stilton has not been produced since the mid-1900s and since 1936 its production has been governed by a handful of large companies that make the cheese. One of the rules applied to this production was that Stilton must be made from pasteurised milk. Thankfully, the production of traditional Stilton made from raw milk has begun again, but it must be sold under the name Stichelton (a slightly ridiculous situation). Apart from Stichelton, Colston Bassett and Cropwell Bishop are also excellent makers of this cheese.

Stilton should not be aggressively strong. Beneath its bronze coloured, crusty rind the interior should be creamy and yellow with not a huge amount of blue veining. The flavour should be both sweet and savoury at the same time.

### Gorgonzola Piccante (PDO since 1996)

From the northern Italian region of Lombardy, comes a blue cheese like no other. Although traditionally matured in caves, this is its only similarity to Roquefort. It is a strong, spicy cheese with a dense interior that is heavily marbled with dark blue/green mould. Made in large 10 kg (22 lb) wheels from the curds of separate milkings, the 3–5 month maturation now mostly takes place in artificial, underground environments with only a few producers still using the traditional mountain caves in the Italian Alps.

Colston Bassett Stilton from Nottinghamshire, England.

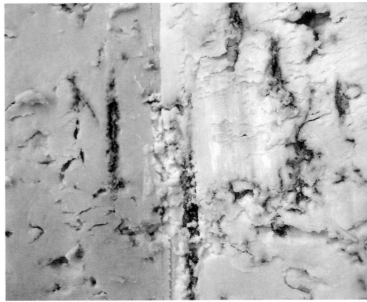

The 'veins' of blue cheese (the vertical lines) are caused by stabbing with needles, which allows air into the cracks, where the mould grows.

Wheels of Stichelton
ageing at Neal's Yard
Dairy in London.

West West, a flagship blue cheese from Parish Hill Creamery in Vermont, USA.

# BLUE CHEESE STRAWS

These are a great way to kick off a dinner party. Try and find a dry crumbly blue for this recipe so that the straws don't become too soft after baking.

**MAKES ABOUT 20 STRAWS**

80 g (2¾ oz) chilled unsalted butter, cubed

150 g (5½ oz/1 cup) plain (all-purpose) flour, plus extra for dusting

200 g (7 oz) blue cheese, crumbled

¼ teaspoon ground cayenne pepper

¼ teaspoon ground cumin

½ teaspoon sea salt flakes, plus extra for sprinkling

1 large egg yolk

Preheat the oven to 180°C (350°F).

Pulse the butter, flour, cheese, spices and salt in a food processor until well combined. Add the egg yolk and continue pulsing until it forms a ball of dough.

Turn the dough out onto a lightly floured work surface and divide the dough in half. Working with one half at a time, roll the dough out to about 5 mm (¼ in) thick. Fold in half and roll out again. Repeat this a couple more times. On the final roll, roll out to a rectangle shape, also 5 mm (¼ in) thick. Use a sharp knife to cut long strips about 1 cm (½ in) wide. Carefully transfer these to baking trays lined with baking paper, arranging them closely together but not touching. Sprinkle with salt flakes and bake for approximately 20–30 minutes or until they just start to brown.

Transfer to wire racks to cool and store in an airtight container for up to 1 week.

# BLUE CHEESE, APPLE AND LEEK PITHIVIER

I love leeks. I especially love them sautéed in butter. Blue cheese and leeks have a very harmonious thing going on. The apple in this can be substituted for pear to give an even sweeter balance to the strong, salty blue cheese.

SERVES 4

50 g (1¾ oz) unsalted butter
1 leek, finely chopped
1 garlic clove, crushed
1 cooking apple, peeled, cored and coarsely grated
1 teaspoon chopped thyme leaves
250 g (9 oz) puff pastry
flour, for dusting
150 g (5½ oz) blue cheese, crumbled (a drier version works better than a soft, creamy version)
1 egg, beaten

Preheat the oven to 210°C (410°F).

Melt the butter in a heavy-based frying pan over medium heat. Add the leek and garlic and sauté for 4–5 minutes or until soft. Remove from the heat, stir in the apple and thyme and set aside.

Divide the pastry in two and roll out each half on a lightly dusted work surface until 5–6 mm (¼ in) thick. Cut out two circles, one slightly bigger than the other (this will be the top).

Place the smaller circle on a baking tray lined with baking paper. Prick all over with a fork. Stir the blue cheese through the cooled leek and apple mixture and spoon it into the centre of the pastry circle, leaving a 2 cm (¾ in) margin from the edge. Brush the pastry margin with a little beaten egg and place the larger pastry circle on top. Use your fingers to press down and seal the two pastry circles together. Cut a 1 cm (½ in) hole in the top of the pastry to allow the steam to escape. Brush the top with beaten egg, then place in the fridge for 30 minutes.

Bake the pithivier for 15 minutes then reduce the oven temperature to 180°C (350°F) and cook for a further 20-25 minutes or until golden brown.

Serve immediately with a green salad on the side.

188

# BLUE CHEESE STEAK SANGERS

This is my ultimate steak sandwich. I love the salty tang of the blue cheese mayo with the charred meatiness of the steak. This is a great mayo recipe to serve with just about any barbecued meat or veggies.

## MAKES 4

4 rump steaks, about
   150–200 g (5½–7 oz) each,
   trimmed of any excess fat
3 tablespoons olive oil
1 large onion, cut into 1 cm
   (½ in) thick rings
4 bread rolls, cut open
large handful of rocket
   (arugula) leaves
2 ripe tomatoes, sliced

## BLUE CHEESE MAYO

3 egg yolks
2 teaspoons white wine
   vinegar
2 teaspoons Dijon mustard
200 ml (7 fl oz) olive oil
180 g (6½ oz) blue cheese,
   crumbled
125 g (4½ oz/½ cup) sour
   cream
finely grated zest of 1 lemon

To make the blue cheese mayo, place the egg yolks, white wine vinegar and mustard in a food processor and blend until light and creamy. While the motor is running, and in a very slow steady stream, gradually add the oil until the mayonnaise becomes thick and pale. Scrape into a bowl and mash in the blue cheese with a fork. Add the sour cream and lemon zest and mix thoroughly. Season with salt and pepper to taste (go easy on the salt because the cheese could be salty) and set aside.

Preheat your barbecue to very hot.

Season the steaks with 2 tablespoons of the olive oil and lots of salt and pepper. Grill for about 3 minutes on each side for medium-rare, or slightly longer if you prefer your steak more well done. Set aside somewhere warm to rest for at least 5 minutes.

Meanwhile, reduce the heat and place the onion rings on the barbecue and drizzle with the remaining olive oil. Using tongs, turn them regularly for a few minutes until charred.

To assemble, spread some blue cheese mayo on the bottom half of each roll. Add a layer of rocket, then place a few fried onion rings on top along with the sliced tomato. Slice the meat on an angle, about 1 cm thick (½ in), and arrange on top of the tomato. Spoon a bit more blue cheese mayo over the steak and top with the other bread roll half.

The blue cheese mayo will keep stored in an airtight container in the fridge for 3–4 days.

# PEAR, WALNUT AND BLUE CHEESE SALAD WITH HONEY DRESSING

Blue cheese and fresh pears are made to go together. They balance each other perfectly in this super simple salad, which is sort of a reinterpretation of the classic Waldorf salad. Serve this on the side with grilled steaks.

SERVES 4

1 small fennel bulb, trimmed and very thinly sliced

large handful of baby rocket (arugula) leaves

1 beurre bosc pear, cored and thinly sliced

130 g (4½ oz) blue cheese, broken into small pieces

60 g (2 oz/½ cup) toasted walnut pieces

HONEY DRESSING

3 teaspoons Dijon mustard

30 ml (1 fl oz) apple cider vinegar

2 tablespoons honey

60 ml (2 fl oz/¼ cup) walnut oil

To make the dressing, whisk the mustard, vinegar and honey in a small bowl. Gradually whisk in the walnut oil. Season with salt and pepper and set aside.

Arrange the salad on a large serving platter starting with the fennel and rocket, then the pear, followed by the blue cheese. Sprinkle the walnuts over the top. Finally, use a spoon to drizzle the dressing over the top of the salad and serve.

# BLUE CHEESE SOUFFLÉS WITH PICKLED CHERRY AND HAZELNUT SALAD

When I was a kid in the 70s, Mum would cook a cheese soufflé for almost every dinner party they had. It was often a disaster and would land on the table deflated and a bit of a damp squib. No matter – it still tasted great!

**SERVES 4**

60 g (2 oz) butter, plus extra for greasing

20 g (¾ oz) finely grated parmesan

2 shallots, finely chopped

35 g (1¼ oz/¼ cup) plain (all-purpose) flour

250 ml (8½ fl oz/1 cup) hot milk

4 egg yolks

75 g (2¾ oz) strong blue cheese, coarsely crumbled

5 egg whites

**PICKLED CHERRY AND HAZELNUT SALAD**

2 teaspoons Dijon mustard

2 tablespoons sherry vinegar

60 ml (2 fl oz/¼ cup) hazelnut oil

200 g (7 oz) celeriac, peeled and julienned, and placed in water with a squeeze of lemon

200 g (7 oz) pickled cherries, pitted

70 g (2½ oz) toasted hazelnuts

Thoroughly grease the inside of four ovenproof ramekins and sprinkle with the grated parmesan (tip any cheese that does not stick into the next ramekin until it is all used up). Tie a collar of baking paper around each ramekin with kitchen string, so that the baking paper stands about 5–6 cm (2–2½ in) proud.

Preheat the oven to 170°C (340°F).

Melt the butter in a saucepan over low heat, being careful not to let it brown. Add the shallot and sauté for a few minutes until translucent. Add the flour and stir for 2 minutes until the mixture comes together. Using a whisk, stir in the milk gradually, whisking as you go to prevent any lumps. Bring to a simmer and stir for 2–3 minutes or until the sauce thickens. Remove from the heat and allow to cool for a few minutes. Add the egg yolks one at a time, stirring well between each addition, until combined. Add the blue cheese and stir through, but keep some of the texture of the cheese rather than melting it completely. Season with salt and pepper.

In a separate bowl, whisk the egg whites until soft peaks form. Using a large metal spoon or spatula, fold one-quarter of the egg white into the cheese mixture, trying to keep the mixture as fluffy as possible. Fold in the remaining egg white.

Divide the mixture evenly among the four ramekins and smooth over the tops using a spatula. Run your finger around the inside of the baking paper collars to pull some of the mixture away from the baking paper; this will help the soufflés rise. Place in the oven for 30 minutes or until the soufflés have risen and are golden on top.

To make the salad, combine the mustard, sherry vinegar and hazelnut oil in a serving bowl and season with salt and pepper. Drain the celeriac and toss through the vinaigrette. Add the pickled cherries and the hazelnuts and mix thoroughly.

Serve the soufflés as soon as they come out of the oven, with the salad on the side.

194

Neal's Yard Dairy at Borough Market, in London. Arguably the best cheese shop in the world.

WORKSOP
BLUE

Made by Joe Schneider at
Welbeck, Nottinghamshire, England

Raw Cow's Milk
Animal Rennet

£14.50/kg

# BLUE CHEESE AND SWEET ONION PIZZA

This is a take on a pizza I once ate at an Italian restaurant in the Japanese city of Sapporo. Although far from the natural home of pizza, the combination of sweet onions and salty blue cheese worked brilliantly and is still one of my 'go-to' pizzas at home.

MAKES 2 LARGE PIZZAS

2 tablespoons olive oil

50 g (1¾ oz) butter

4 large onions, thinly sliced

1 teaspoon salt

2 tablespoons soft brown sugar

2 tablespoons balsamic vinegar

2 pizza bases (see page 136)

350 g (12½ oz) strong blue cheese, crumbled

small handful of rocket (arugula) leaves

Heat the olive oil in a heavy-based frying pan over medium heat. Add the butter, onion and salt and reduce the heat to very low. Cook slowly, stirring frequently, for 20 minutes or until the onion is soft and starting to turn golden. Add the sugar and half of the vinegar and continue cooking slowly for a further 10 minutes, stirring regularly to prevent the onions from sticking. Set aside to cool.

Follow the instructions on page 136 to make the pizza bases. This recipe calls for 2 bases, so you will only need one-third of the ingredients.

Preheat the oven to 240°C (460°F).

Sprinkle the caramelised onion and the blue cheese evenly over the pizza bases.

Bake each pizza for 10–12 minutes. Toss the rocket leaves in the remaining balsamic vinegar and pile on top of each pizza.

198

# PARISH HILL CREAMERY

Peter Dixon is a kindred spirit. He is a tall, lanky Vermonter who speaks slowly and authoritatively, but with the air of inquisitiveness of someone who is always keen to learn more.

Rachel and Peter Dixon

As a dairy foods consultant and artisan cheesemaker, Peter Dixon draws on more than 30 years of cheesemaking, as well as 20 years of consulting with people engaged in or interested in making cheese and dairy products. Peter works with dairy farmers and cheesemakers to help them improve their milk processing businesses and, as such, has been a guiding hand in the development of the American artisan cheese industry over the past three decades.

In 2013, Peter started Parish Hill Creamery, a small seasonal cheese business where he produces handmade raw milk cheeses with his wife Rachel and sister Alex. Parish Hill Creamery allows Peter to hone his craft and pursue his passion for retaining terroir in cheese.

**WHEN YOU LOOK AT THE ARTISAN CHEESE INDUSTRY IN AMERICA, DOES IT GIVE YOU A SENSE OF PRIDE?**
*Yes, it does give me a great sense of pride. The growth of the cheese industry in America parallels my own career somewhat. When I first got into cheese in 1983, I was something of a pioneer. Since then I have worked with many people who are kindred souls, committed people with integrity and passion, and who have been responsible for the development of the industry. It has been very rewarding to see those people progress.*

*Another thing that makes me proud is the access to great education people in the cheese industry now have. This has made a huge difference. If you want to get into the cheese industry, as a maker or a monger, there are now lots of really great courses available. The result of this is much better cheese, as cheesemakers can't get away with making bad cheese, because cheesemongers and consumers are well educated and demand high quality. Thirty years ago, there was very little American cheese sold in shops, and almost all of it was cow's milk and really only a couple of varieties. Now, most good cheesemongers will have about half of their range coming from the States.*

**WHAT ARE SOME OF THE FRUSTRATIONS YOU HAVE ABOUT THE REGULATIONS THAT NEED TO BE COMPLIED WITH WHEN MAKING CHEESE IN THE US?**
*The big issue I have at the moment is the standard used by the Food and Drug Administration (FDA) for non-toxogenic E. coli. This is fine for pasteurised cheese but the same standard is also applied to raw milk cheese. There is absolutely no scientific basis for this standard, and the officials are not trained properly in cheesemaking technology.*

Idyll, a raw cooked curd cheese.

Humble, a semi-hard raw milk cheese.

I would much prefer the FDA take a more reasonable approach to this subject.

### INDIVIDUAL STATES APPLY THE FDA REGULATIONS DIFFERENTLY – DOES THAT MAKE IT DIFFICULT TO BE A COHESIVE INDUSTRY? WHY DID YOU CHOOSE VERMONT TO MAKE CHEESE?

*Yes. Again, I think the reason for this is a lack of appropriate training, so the application of the regulations is sometimes more arbitrary than sensible. In Vermont, it seems to be better than other states but I make cheese here because I am a Vermonter. I'm just lucky!*

### YOU HAVE SPENT MANY YEARS ADVISING OTHER CHEESEMAKERS AND HELPING THEM DEVELOP MANY GREAT CHEESES. WHY DID YOU WANT TO START YOUR OWN CHEESERY AND WHAT ARE YOUR GOALS FOR PARISH HILL CREAMERY?

*Whenever I worked for other people, I would always think, 'when is my next chance to make my own cheese?' In my heart I am a cheesemaker but I got into education out of necessity and circumstance.*

*Parish Hill Creamery is all about capturing terroir. We keep things as local as possible to achieve this. We use raw milk, we make our own starters, we are starting to make our own rennet and I want to start culturing our own moulds.*

### I AM INTERESTED IN THE NOTION THAT INDUSTRIAL CHEESEMAKING IS ALL ABOUT CONTROL AND TRADITIONAL CHEESEMAKING IS MORE ABOUT RELINQUISHING THAT CONTROL. IF YOU ARE WANTING TO MAKE CHEESE WITH TRUE REGIONAL CHARACTER, WHAT ARE THE MOST IMPORTANT THINGS TO KEEP CONTROL OF?

*You need to control the ingredients. The only way to preserve terroir in cheese is through raw milk. Using raw milk retains the spirit of the soil, the feed, the animal and the geography. Raw milk is the essence of the land and is the most genuine way to claim local character.*

201

# SEMI-HARD CHEESES

This is where cheese starts to get serious. Semi-hard cheeses tend to reflect the seasonality of the milk from which they are made, and also the influence of maturation.

Semi-hard cheeses are made differently to soft cheeses in that the curd is usually cut smaller to allow more whey to escape. The curd is also stirred for longer, again, to facilitate a drier result. Rind development is critical in the maturation stage. Rinds can be anything from a sticky, smeary bacterial rind such as the rind of a raclette, to the dry, crusty, mouldy rind of an aged Tomme, or even the cloth-bandaged rind of farmhouse cheddar, which forms an environment for a complex flora of moulds and bacteria to grow.

## BENCHMARK SEMI-HARD CHEESES

### West Country Farmhouse Cheddar (PDO since 1996)

Cheddar is worth a special mention here, not just because it has become an almost ubiquitous cheese variety around the world, but because real cheddar is little understood and even less commonly produced. Its production also has a couple of very interesting steps that are completely unique.

The vast majority of cheeses named cheddar are dumbed-down, mass-produced, rindless versions made around the world in big rectangular blocks that are vacuum-packed and aged in cool rooms. Cheddar became corrupted after WWII when the bog-standard, mass-production of cheddar was introduced in the UK and North America. By comparison, the real thing comes only from England's West Country, where only 12 producers are recognised. They make a cheese which is cloth-wrapped and often made using old strains of bacteria (known as 'pint starters', which are based on traditional local microflora) and calves' rennet, which help produce the complex, round flavours. The curd undergoes a special acidification

step called 'cheddaring' where it is drained and formed into blocks, which are stacked and turned by hand for one hour. This important process also helps to develop the texture by binding the crumbly lumps of curd into pliable slabs and is critical to producing the dry texture of the finished cheese. These slabs of curd are then milled and salt is mixed directly through the curd, which assists in arresting the development of further acidity. The curd is then pressed overnight before being wrapped in muslin (cheesecloth) – often applied with the use of lard – and transferred to the ageing room. These wheels, which traditionally weigh 18 kg (40 lb), are aged for a minimum of 12 months.

### Reblochon AOC (PDO since 1996)

This is a cheese I hold on a pedestal, as tasting farm-made Reblochon for the first time was one of my early defining moments as a cheesemaker. When you get a good one, this cheese has it all: a wonderful, silky texture encased in a damp, leathery rind and a deeply satisfying, funky flavour that is milky, buttery and also powerfully meaty at the same time. Made in the Savoie and Haute-Savoie departments of France, Reblochon is made from the milk of traditional mountain cattle breeds Abondance, Tarine and Montbéliarde in small 500 g (1 lb 2 oz) rounds about 15 cm (6 in) diameter and 3–4 cm (1¼–1½ in) thick. It is mostly made in co-operatives but farm-made versions (usually only produced during spring and autumn) are well worth seeking out if you can.

### Manchego PDO (PDO since 1996)

It is hard to imagine how such a fully flavoured cheese could spring from the hot, dry, rocky plains of Spain's La Mancha region. It is here that the local Manchega sheep are tended to. These hardy sheep provide the herbaceous milk that gives this cheese its flavour almost year round. Traditionally, the curds were drained in baskets made from woven reeds which left a pattern on the exterior of the cheese. These days only the most artisanal makers still use these baskets with most opting for plastic versions. The cheese is shaped into 2 kg (4 lb 6 oz) rounds and aged from 3–12 months, with the ivory curd developing stronger flavours as it ages.

### Cantal AOC (PDO since 1996)

Reported to be one of the oldest cheeses in France and possibly a distant forefather to English cheddar, Cantal comes from the Auvergne region. Although production has now been taken over by big producers who make smaller, faster maturing wheels, the best Cantal is made in huge, traditional 45 kg (99 lb) drum-shaped wheels that age slowly in underground rooms. Two other AOC cheeses that are similar in style and geography are Laguiole and Salers, and high quality versions of both are often easier to track down.

### Ossau-Iraty AOC (PDO since 2003)

This is a seasonally produced semi-hard cheese from the French Basque region. It is made from the milk of Manech ewes and formed into 4 kg (8 lb 13 oz) wheels. The rind, developed over a 6–9 month maturation period, is a fine, silty grey-coloured mould, which gives the cheese a nutty, earthy character. Most production of this cheese is now exported and therefore made from pasteurised milk, but raw milk versions are superior and easy to find in Europe.

### Tomme

Tomme is a style of cheese that is common throughout the mountainous regions of France, Italy and Switzerland. It can be made with cow's, sheep's or goat's milk. All Tommes have a couple of things in common: they are all quite small, semi-hard cheeses meaning they often age at a faster rate and exhibit developed characteristics that belie their real age; and they all have a natural rind that contains indigenous microflora that further drives flavour and complexity into the cheese.

Tomme de Savoie is probably the best known version but others to look out for include the Italian Toma and Tomme de Montagne, which is a generic description for this style of cheese when it is made high in the French and Swiss Alps.

205

# HOW TO MAKE SEMI-HARD CHEESE

Making a semi-hard cheese successfully at home is not difficult, but it does require a bit of care when it comes to the maturation.

HERE IS WHAT YOU
WILL NEED:
8 litres (2.1 gallons) fresh unhomogenised full-cream (whole) milk

¼ teaspoon commercial bacterial starter culture or 1 tablespoon 'live' yoghurt

thermometer

10 litre (2.6 gallon) stainless-steel stockpot/double boiler (or equivalent)

slotted serving spoon

syringe to measure the rennet

2–3 ml (¼ fl oz) rennet

long-bladed serrated knife (a bread knife is fine)

20 litre (5.3 gallon) plastic box with lid (this will be your cheese cave)

wire rack to fit inside plastic box

2 cheese hoops about 20 cm (8 in) diameter

salt

### Preparing the starter (the day before)

In a small saucepan boil, then cool, 200 ml (7 fl oz) of the milk. Transfer to a sterilised, dry glass jar with a tight fitting lid. Add ¼ teaspoon of commercial starter culture or 1 tablespoon of 'live' yoghurt and stir well. Screw the lid on and store the jar at 25°C–30°C (77°F–86°F) until the mixture thickens to the consistency of yoghurt (approximately 12–24 hours). If this does not happen, you will need to start again with some fresh starter. Your starter will store in the fridge for a couple of days until needed.

### Preparing the milk

If you are going to pasteurise the milk, follow the instructions on page 104, then cool it back down to 33°C (91°F). If you are using fresh, raw milk, place it in your stockpot and place over a low heat until it reaches 33°C (91°F). Alternatively, heat the milk over a water bath. Stir regularly with your slotted spoon to make sure the milk doesn't burn or catch on the bottom.

Remove the pot from the heat and place in a bowl of water (or use your sink) heated to 35°C (95°F). You want to keep the temperature of the milk between 32°C–35°C (90°F–95°F) while you continue to make the cheese. Adjust the temperature of the water bath to warm or cool your milk as required.

### Add the starter culture

Add the prepared starter culture and mix well through the milk. Cover your stockpot and set aside for 75 minutes.

### Renneting

Use the syringe to measure out the rennet in a small bowl. Dilute the rennet with 50 ml (1¾ fl oz) water. Gently stir into the milk with an up and down motion for at least 1 minute. Once you are satisfied that the rennet is completely stirred through evenly, you need to use your slotted spoon to stop the milk from moving around in your stockpot. Cover the stockpot again and leave to set for 60 minutes or until you get a 'clean break' (see below).

### Testing for a clean break

Slide your finger into the curd at a 45 degree angle and lift it up towards the surface. If the curd breaks cleanly around your finger and whey runs into the crack left behind, you have a 'clean break'. The curd is now ready to be cut. If it still seems a bit sloppy, give it another 10 minutes.

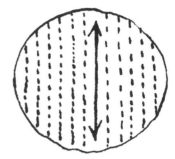

First cut

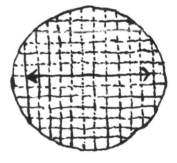

Second cut

## Cutting the curd

Use the illustrations at right as a guide to cut the curd into 1 cm (½ in) cubes. Leave to stand for 20 minutes to set.

## Stirring the curds

Using extremely clean hands or your slotted spoon, turn all the curds over gently for 3 minutes. Try and bring the curds on the bottom up to the top – they will be very fragile at this stage so go easy – you don't want to smash the curds. Any larger curds that come up from the bottom may be cut at this stage. Continue stirring for 30 minutes.

## Preparing the curd

After the final stir, let the curds rest and sink into the whey. Using a glass or ladle, scoop out about 60% of the whey and discard (or keep it to make ricotta, see page 116). After the whey has been removed, give the curds a gentle stir to keep them from knitting back together. You are trying to keep all the curds separate from each other.

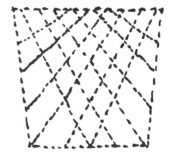

Horizontal cut

### Filling the hoops

Making sure that your cheese cave, wire rack and hoops have been sterilised (I sit everything in boiling water), set up your cave with the wire rack sitting on the bottom of the box with your hoops on top. Pour the curds and remaining whey evenly into your hoops. Use the palm of your hand to press down on the curds to squeeze out as much whey as possible.

### Turning the hoops

Turn the cheeses over inside the hoops and continue pressing down on the curds for a further 10–15 minutes. Turn them again after an hour or so and leave to drain overnight in the box with the lid on.

### Salting the cheese

The following morning the young cheese will have firmed up and should pull away easily from the hoop edges. This indicates that the cheese can now be removed for salting.

Take the cheeses out of the hoops and lightly sprinkle salt over the top of each cheese and leave to stand for 15–30 minutes. Turn the cheeses over, lightly sprinkle the bottom and sides with more salt and let stand for a further 15–30 minutes. You only want to use 1–2 teaspoons salt per cheese. Shake off any excess salt and return the cheeses to the cheese cave. Place the lid back on and keep the box at 15°C (60°F) overnight.

### Ageing the cheese

Your cheeses will now spend the next 2–6 months maturing in the cheese cave. They should be kept at a constant temperature between 10°C–14°C (50°F–57°F), and turned and rubbed back with a clean cloth or kitchen towel every week or so to control the growth of indigenous moulds.

### Monitor the cheese weekly

The only other problem at this stage is humidity – or generally, a lack of it. You want a high humidity, especially to start with, so look for a slight condensation on the inside of the cheese cave – add a damp towel to increase the humidity, if necessary. If there is excessive condensation on the lid of the box, this can drip onto the cheese causing a yellowish slime. If this happens, remove the lid, wipe away the moisture and replace the lid, leaving it slightly ajar. Check the bottom of the box for excessive moisture. You may need to replace the damp towel if this occurs.

### When is it ready to eat?

This is up to you but I would recommend giving them at least 2 months and anywhere up to 6 months. The cheeses should weigh between 500 g–1 kg (1 lb 2 oz–2 lb 3 oz).

208

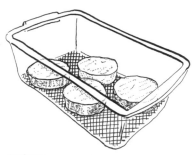

**NOTE** Keep a lid on it so it stays humid.

## THE DARK ART OF MATURATION

I joke that I can teach someone everything I know about making cheese in about two hours. But it would take a lifetime to teach them the art of maturation. This is the process where young, uninteresting cheese is transformed into something that can be so beautiful it makes you weep with joy.

Real cheese is a living, breathing thing that literally changes on a daily basis – a soft, surface-ripened cheese, for example, can have a window of perfection of just a few days. The maturation of cheese is a skillful act of balancing literally dozens of factors, the most important of which are temperature and humidity.

### Temperature

The ideal temperature range for real cheese is 10°C–15°C (50°F–59°F). Any lower than this and the microflora in the cheese will become dormant and the cheese will not develop to its potential. A higher temperature causes the fats in the cheese to break down and the cheese will become oily and start to smell rotten.

Modern cheese, by contrast, is designed to be stable at very low temperatures so that supermarkets can maximise shelf life.

### Humidity

The rind is the vital interface between the cheese and the outside environment. The moulds, bacteria and yeasts on the rind all require a high humidity environment between 75–90% to thrive. In traditional caves this level of humidity occurs naturally, but in modern facilities it needs to be artificially created.

# WELSH RAREBIT

It's the simple things in life that are the best. Take cheese on toast for example. When it is made with care, simplicity and the best ingredients, it can be the best meal you remember. Welsh rarebit is a great example of this.

Getting the ingredients right for Welsh rarebit is important. Although traditionally it was made with Welsh caerphilly, these days most recipes call for cheddar or Lancashire cheese, and I tend to agree – caerphilly just doesn't pack a big enough punch. And whether you add stout or cider to the mix is up to you, both are traditional, so let your taste buds decide.

SERVES 2

30 g (1 oz) butter
3 tablespoons stout or
    dry cider
1 teaspoon hot English
    mustard
2 teaspoons Worcestershire
    sauce
200 g (7 oz) mild cheddar or
    Lancashire cheese, grated
2 thick slices multigrain
    (wholegrain) bread
2 egg yolks

Melt the butter in a small saucepan over a low heat, then add the stout, mustard and Worcestershire sauce.

Add the cheese and stir until completely melted and combined. Remove from the heat and allow to cool for 10 minutes.

Preheat the grill (broiler) and toast the bread on both sides. While it is toasting, beat the egg yolks into the cheese mixture. Pour the cheese onto the toast and place back under the grill until the cheese is bubbling and golden.

210

# ALIGOT

Aligot may just be the ultimate comfort food for me – a combination of mashed potato, melted cheese and garlic. It comes from the Auvergne region of France, in the Massif Central, where cheeses such as young Tommes, Cantal or Laguiole are used, but you can get away with almost any young, semi-hard cheese for this dish.

SERVES 6

900 g (2 lb) floury potatoes, peeled and cut into quarters
2 tablespoons crème fraîche
60 g (2 oz) butter
2 garlic cloves, crushed
600 g (1 lb 5 oz) semi-hard cheese, coarsely grated

Bring the potatoes to the boil in a large saucepan of salted water, reduce to a simmer and cook until they are tender and cooked through. Drain and mash the potatoes.

Add the crème fraîche, butter and garlic and return the pan to a low heat. Stir to combine, then gradually add the cheese, one handful at a time, letting it melt and stirring to combine before you add the next handful. When all of the cheese is melted and stirred through, season with salt and pepper and serve.

213

# EGG, BACON AND CHEDDAR PIES

I have a bunch of mates that I regularly go fishing with and it has become an expectation that I will bring a batch of these pies onboard every time we go out. I once left a box of them at home, so a new course was set for my house on Bruny Island. I had to wade in and walk up to my house to fetch them – they are that good!

**MAKES 6**

6 rashers (slices) bacon, rind removed
6 eggs
12 x 1 cm (½ in) cubes cheddar cheese, or other semi-hard cheese
6 parsley sprigs

**SHORTCRUST PASTRY**

340 g (12 oz) plain (all-purpose) flour, plus extra for dusting
150 g (5½ oz) chilled butter, chopped
2–3 tablespoons iced water

To make the shortcrust pastry, put the flour and butter in a food processor and pulse until the mixture resembles breadcrumbs. Gradually add the water, a little at a time, until the mixture starts to come together. Turn out onto a clean work surface and bring the dough together to form a ball. Wrap in plastic wrap and refrigerate for 30 minutes.

Preheat the oven to 190°C (375°F). Grease a 6-hole muffin tin.

Roll out the pastry on a lightly floured work surface to 3–4 mm (¼ in) thick. Cut out 6 circles big enough to line the muffin holes. Line each hole with a circle of pastry, being careful to push the pastry into the corners and not tear it. You can trim any excess pastry if you like your tarts neat and tidy, but I am not that fussed. Set aside.

Fry the bacon until it starts to brown but is not too crispy. Place a rasher of bacon in the bottom of each pie shell (you might need to fold it over a bit). Break in a whole egg and top with a couple of cubes of cheese and a sprig of parsley. Finish with a couple of grinds of black pepper.

Bake in the oven for 25–30 minutes. Remove the pies from the tin immediately and allow to cool a little before serving.

# MACARONI CHEESE

In my house we just call it 'cheesy pasta' and it's at the top of the most requested dinner list.

SERVES 6

400 g (14 oz) macaroni

50 g (1¾ oz) butter

25 g (1 oz) plain (all-purpose) flour

450 ml (15 fl oz) full-cream (whole) milk

200 g (7 oz) semi-hard cheese, grated (use whatever you have on hand)

½ teaspoon seeded mustard

pinch of freshly grated nutmeg

40 g (1½ oz/½ cup) fresh breadcrumbs

1 tablespoon grated parmesan

2 teaspoons finely chopped thyme leaves

Preheat the oven to 200°C (400°F).

In a large stockpot, cook the pasta in plenty of boiling salted water until al dente.

While the pasta is cooking, melt half the butter in a heavy-based saucepan over medium heat and stir in the flour. Cook for a couple of minutes, stirring, and then gradually whisk in the milk, whisking constantly until the sauce thickens. Remove from the heat and stir through the grated semi-hard cheese, mustard and nutmeg.

Drain the pasta and transfer to an ovenproof dish. Pour the cheese sauce over the top and stir through. Melt the remaining butter in a small pan. Remove from the heat and transfer to a small bowl. Add the breadcrumbs, parmesan and thyme and mix well to combine. Sprinkle this over the top of the pasta.

Bake in the oven for about 15–20 minutes or until the crust is golden brown.

## CHEESE AND WOOD

I have long held a fascination with the relationship between cheese and the wood that it sits upon. Wood has served cheesemakers well for millennia – not just as maturing-room shelves, but also as vats, buckets, ladles and churns. But like most traditional practices, in recent years its use has come under attack from scientists and regulators because of wood's ability to harbour bacteria, even though it has never been documented to have caused any food-borne disease outbreak in the US, Europe or Australia. Stupidly, it is precisely its ability to harbour bacteria that makes it an essential material used in cheesemaking and maturation. Cantal, Salers and Ragusano (all European PDO cheeses) still use wooden vats for their production, and none of these cheeses have starter culture added to them – it is the natural bacteria that resides in the wood that safely and efficiently inoculates the milk with indigenous lactic acid bacteria to start the fermentation. This has been the way for hundreds of years and is only now coming into question. Like I said … stupid.

In the French Alps, spruces and firs contribute a regional flavour to the rind of the cheese. On Bruny Island we use Huon Pine, a native to Tasmania, which imparts a smoky characteristic that is unique to its location.

An aged semi-hard raw sheep's milk cheese from Vermont Shepherd, Vermont.

Wallabout, a raw milk tomme-style cheese made at Spring Brook Farm in Reading, Vermont. Here it is being finished on oregon timber at Crown Finish Caves in Brooklyn, New York.

# CAULIFLOWER CHEESE

When I was at school, I occasionally ate lunch with my mates who were boarders. They were served up meals in what was essentially an army mess hall, but with the posh moniker of DaCosta Hall. I remember only two things (I wish I didn't): the custard and the cauliflower cheese. They could be easily confused. Both were pale, lumpy, steaming trays of gloop. The only way to distinguish between the two was the sulphorous, composting vegetable-matter smell of the cauliflower.

Years later, when I became a cheesemaker, I would taste my first real camembert: a farmhouse, raw milk cheese made in Normandy in France. It was life changing. The flavour was incredible. But the remarkable thing was, it took me straight back to DaCosta. The cheese and that horrible, overcooked cauliflower had the same flavour. But this time I loved it!

This dish is classic English comfort food. But they usually boil the whole head of cauliflower, cover it in white sauce and then bake it in the oven. Here is how I think it should be done.

SERVES 2 AS A MAIN COURSE
OR 6 AS A SIDE DISH
900 ml (30½ fl oz) full-cream (whole) milk
1 small onion, peeled but kept whole
2 fresh bay leaves
100 g (3½ oz) butter
50 g (1¾ oz) plain (all-purpose) flour
freshly grated nutmeg
250 g (9 oz) mix of grated semi-hard cheeses – choose something strong-flavoured
50 ml (1¾ fl oz) thick (double/heavy) cream
1 medium cauliflower

In a small saucepan, bring the milk, onion and bay leaves to a gentle simmer. Remove from the heat and set aside to cool. Remove and discard the onion and bay leaves and season with salt and pepper.

Melt half the butter in a saucepan over medium heat and stir in the flour with a whisk. Keep stirring for about two minutes before gradually adding the milk. Whisk constantly to ensure that there are no lumps. Reduce the heat, add a sprinkling of grated nutmeg, 200 g (7 oz) of the grated cheese and the cream, and stir until the cheese is completely melted and the sauce thickens. Remove from the heat.

Preheat the grill (broiler).

Bring a large pot of salted water to the boil. Cut the florets from the main stalk of the cauliflower and boil the florets for 3–5 minutes, depending on their size. Drain the cauliflower and set aside.

Melt the remaining butter in an ovenproof frying pan over high heat. Toss in the cauliflower and fry until it is lightly browned. Pour the cheese sauce over the top and sprinkle with the remaining grated cheese. Place under the grill until the top is golden and bubbling.

# BEST-EVER CHEESE BISCUITS

My mate Matthew's mum makes these brilliant little biscuits. Barbara rolls the dough out and cuts them into squares but I like to form the dough into rolls and slice off circles. Make double the recipe and keep a roll of the dough in the freezer to pull out and bake when friends drop by for unexpected drinks.

MAKES ABOUT 24

170 g (6 oz) chilled unsalted cultured butter, cut into cubes
250 g (9 oz/1⅔ cups) plain (all-purpose) flour
pinch of salt
good pinch of ground cayenne pepper
150 g (5½ oz) strong-flavoured cheddar, finely grated

Put the butter and flour in a bowl and rub them together using your fingertips, until they resemble breadcrumbs. You can also do this in a food processor, if you prefer. Add the salt and cayenne, then knead in the cheese until combined. Roll into a ball.

Tear off a couple of sheets of baking paper, about 30 cm (12 in) square. Divide the dough in half and place each half in the centre of each piece of baking paper. Roll into a sausage shape, using the paper as a casing. Twist the ends to seal and place in the fridge for an hour to chill and harden (if you are going to store one of the rolls in the freezer, wrap well in plastic wrap first).

Preheat the oven to 200°C (400°F).

Slice discs off of the dough, about 7–8 mm (⅓ in) thick, and place on a baking tray lined with baking paper. Bake for 15 minutes or until they are golden. Turn out onto a wire rack to cool before storing in an airtight container.

222

# WESTCOMBE DAIRY

The approach to Westcombe Dairy takes you through some of the most beautiful farming land in England and villages with some of the best names imaginable, like Wookey Hole, Shepton Mallet and Witham Friary.

Tom Calver, Westcombe Cheddar.

Cheddar has been made on the farm since 1890. Originally owned by the Bricknell family, cheese production was small and artisanal until the 1970s when the decision was made to expand and move into industrial cheese production. Cloth-matured wheels were replaced with large blocks of vacuum-packed cheese. In the late 80s, Richard Calver, who had been a partner in the business for 20 years, realised that quality cheesemaking was where their strengths lay and set about returning Westcombe to the production of traditional raw milk farmhouse cheddar.

Richard's son Tom took the reins in 2008 and, using his skills gained as a chef, completed the move back to tradition, where they are now able to concentrate on producing some of the best cheddar in England.

224

**TOM, YOU ARE ESSENTIALLY ONE OF A HANDFUL OF GUARDIANS OF A CHEESE WHICH IS FAMOUS THROUGHOUT THE WORLD. NO OTHER CHEESE IS MORE IMPORTANT TO THE ENGLISH CULTURE THAN CHEDDAR. HOW DOES THIS MAKE YOU FEEL?**

*I am really happy to keep traditional cheddar going. Cheddar has got a bad reputation for being bland and boring but when you make it traditionally, it enters another world.*

**LIKE ME, YOU FIRST CAME TO CHEESEMAKING THROUGH BEING A CHEF. WHAT MADE YOU WANT TO LEAVE THE STOVE AND SPECIALISE IN MAKING CHEESE? WHAT CHEFS' SKILLS HAVE YOU BROUGHT TO CHEESEMAKING?**

*I wanted to try and capture a place in a flavour and cheese helps me do that. You learn how to taste when you cook professionally and that's a great help when trying to understand the variance in flavour that you get in cheese.*

**IS THE SPECIFIC TERROIR OF SOMERSET STILL INTACT, DESPITE THE MODERNISATION OF AGRICULTURE? WHAT CHARACTERISTICS IN YOUR CHEESE DO YOU ATTRIBUTE DIRECTLY TO TERROIR?**

*We attribute most of our characteristics to terroir. I think that terroir is always evolving, so yes, it is intact, but I also like to think that with more knowledge we can farm in a way that is even more conscious of the impact the land has on our cheese.*

**WHAT ROLE DOES THE CLOTH PLAY IN YOUR CHEDDAR?**

*The cloth is protection. It stops the cheddar from drying out too quickly during maturation.*

Stirring salt through the milled cheddar curds.

Westcombe Dairy cheesemaker Jason Coles.

*Milk. Made.*

# COOKED CURD CHEESES

These are cheeses I love. Not only for their complex, umami-rich flavour that is intensified through maturation, but also because they are still commonly made in the Alpine regions, employing low-level technology that has been proven over centuries of cheesemaking.

The defining feature of cooked curd cheeses is that their curds (which are finely cut to increase the surface areas for whey to escape) are heated in the whey to around 50°C (122°F). This application of heat not only causes the curds to shrink, forcing out even more whey and producing a drier, harder cheese that can sustain longer periods of maturation (useful when you are making cheese in the isolation of high altitudes), but it also enables the lactose to caramelise at around 48°C (118°F), producing the sweet, nutty characters so common in these cheeses. Cooked curd cheeses are usually pressed in hoops and drained overnight to force out any remaining whey. This dry curd, along with their usual large forms, enables them to be aged for several years.

## BENCHMARK COOKED CURD CHEESES

Around the world there are many benchmark cheeses from this family – here are a few of my significant favourites.

### Parmigiano Reggiano DOC (PDO since 1996)
Working in some of the great cheese shops around the world afforded me one of the greatest sensory joys possible – splitting a wheel of aged Parmigiano Reggiano. To smell the intense aromas as they leave the inside of the cheese for the first time is an incredible experience. The sweet, savoury flavour and the granular structure of the curd that often provides a crystalline crunch in older wheels are the hallmarks of this great cheese. Despite the enormity of its production and popularity, this cheese is still largely made on farms by small producers or co-operatives,

and uses whey starters made in-house. However, the agriculture has changed for this cheese over the centuries with the traditional breeds of cows – the Modenese and Vacche Rossa – being sadly replaced with the more ubiquitous Holstein.

Often considered the lesser equal to Parmigiano Reggiano, Grana Padano is similar in style but comes from a much greater geographical area. As a general rule, production and maturation quality is less rigorously controlled than Parmigiano Reggiano, making the chance of a low quality wheel more common.

### Emmentaler (PGI since 1996)
The whopper of the cheese world, weighing in at 100 kg (220 lb), Emmentaler is a member of the gruyère family, with the distinct difference that during the early months of unusually warm maturation, bacteria is added to the milk to create gas and form holes in the curd. Emmentaler is largely a product of co-operative dairies throughout the Swiss canton of Bern, but it is also made over the border in the French Alps. Look for cheeses with a Grand Cru label that indicate smaller production houses and traditional agriculture.

### Beaufort AOC (PDO since 2003)
Another outstanding member of the gruyère stable, raw milk Beaufort is made in thick wheels that weigh in at 50–60 kg (110–132 lb) from the milk of the Tarine and Abondance breeds of cow in the valleys and mountains of the Savoie region of France. Cheeses marked as Beaufort d'alpage are especially sought after as these are produced on a very small scale in mountain huts during the summer months when the

cows are walked high into the mountains to graze the very seasonal pastures. Maturation is normally outsourced to affineurs, but these are still small artisanal operations.

## Comté AOC (PDO since 1996)

Not just one of the most wonderful of all cheeses, Comté is also the product of an impressive system of controlled production and maturation, ensuring that it is one of the most consistently high quality and popular cheeses in France. Cheeses are made on-farm or by local small co-operatives called fruitière throughout the Franche-Comté. Maturation is almost exclusively carried out by large affineurs (often with the use of robots to turn and rub the large wheels) who take the cheese at only one or two weeks of age.

The Alpine breeds of Montbéliarde and Simmental are critical to the quality of Comté, which is made exclusively with raw milk, and the method of agriculture is strictly governed to preserve milk quality and terroir. The milk is pre-ripened by storing it above 10°C (50°F), which helps develop flavour and acidity. Production takes place in copper vats with the use of whey starters from the previous day's production.

The complicated and carefully controlled affinage of Comté is paramount to its quality and to visit one of the large caves, where up to 100,000 wheels are matured, is a sight to behold. The two best affineurs to look out for are Jean-Charles Arnaud's Fort des Rousses and Marcel Petite's Fort St. Antoine.

## Gouda (PGI since 2010)

The Dutch have an impeccable cheesemaking pedigree and central to this long history is Gouda. This cheese is much more than the brightly coloured supermarket version. Production of Gouda, from the region between the cities of Amsterdam, Rotterdam and Utrecht has been carried out on farms since the 1400s. These days much of the production is industrialised (the cheeses are commonly painted with a kind of plastic to prevent mould growing on the rind) but artisanal production still exists and if you

are lucky enough to find it, expect an unparalleled experience. The curd of this cheese is washed with water to remove lactose that might later become acidic. The result is a powerful sweetness that fills your mouth. Look for cheeses that have been aged for at least a year.

A typical copper vat used in mountain cheesemaking.

Wheels of Comté at the prestigious Fort des Rousses, in Jura, France.

# CHEESE FRICOS

Trust the Italians to take that little bit of cheese that always oozes out of your toasted cheese sandwich when cooking to become a crunchy, cheesy morsel, and turn it into an entire dish. This is perhaps the simplest recipe in the book. And the best.

MAKES ABOUT 25

500 g (1 lb 2 oz/5 cups) finely grated hard cheese (the Italians use Montasio, a delicious hard, cooked curd cheese from the north of Italy. Any hard cheese will do, or even better, mix it up)

1 tablespoon plain (all-purpose) flour

In a mixing bowl, combine the cheese and flour, ensuring that the flour completely coats all of the cheese.

Heat your heaviest frying pan over a low–medium heat. A non-stick pan works well and a well-seasoned cast-iron pan is even better. If you don't have either of these, lightly coat your pan with oil spray to stop the cheese from sticking.

Take a heaped tablespoon of the cheese mixture and sprinkle it in the pan to form a circle about 10 cm (4 in) in diameter. You can use an egg ring to form the circle but you will need to remove it before the cheese melts and sticks to it. After a minute or two the cheese will start to melt and bond together like lace. When the edges start to look golden brown, carefully flip the disc with a spatula and cook for a further minute on the other side.

Immediately remove the disc with the spatula and drape over a rolling pin or laid-down wine bottle to cool. As soon as it cools it will keep this shape.

Repeat this process with the remaining cheese mixture. Keeping the pan at the right temperature is critical – if it gets too hot, let it cool before you proceed. Store your fricos in an airtight container for up to a week. Serve as a beer snack or crumble over salads.

# FROMAGE FORT

This is a bit of an acquired taste. 'Fromage fort' sounds more delicious than 'strong cheese' but that's pretty much what it is. When you travel around France, especially in the Rhône-Alpes, you will see it on sale in fromageries and from market cheese vendors. I don't know when the practice began, but fromage fort became a way for cheese sellers to use up their 'bits' of leftover or unsaleable cheese. Any cheese can be added to the mix along with a healthy splash of booze and spices, and the result is definitely greater than the sum of its parts.

In the good old days, kitchens in the Rhône-Alpes would have a jar of this keeping warm near the stove, presumably undergoing some kind of continual fermentation. Cheese would be added as available to 'feed the beast'. That's all a bit hard these days. This recipe uses a food processor and a fridge, but it's still good. Use it as a dip or spread on food to add a cheesy kick.

MAKES 500 G
(1 LB 2 OZ/2 CUPS)

500 g (1 lb 2 oz) cheese, rind
    removed, cut into cubes –
    can be any soft, blue or
    aged cheese, depending
    on your preference
125 ml (4 fl oz/½ cup) dry
    white wine
50 ml (1¾ fl oz) brandy
50 g (1¾ oz) unsalted butter,
    softened
2 garlic cloves, finely
    chopped
small handful finely
    chopped herbs such as
    parsley, sage and thyme

Throw the whole lot into a food processor, season with freshly ground black pepper and blend until combined. Try and keep a bit of texture instead of blending to a smooth paste.

Transfer to an airtight container or a sterilised jar. It will keep in the fridge for up to a month.

236

# CROQUE MONSIEUR

It gives me a wry smile to think that of all the incredible dishes the French have contributed to the world of gastronomy there is none more famous than their version of the humble toasted ham and cheese sandwich. That said, they do do it better than anyone else. There are a hundred ways to make croque monsieur, with variations including the use of béchamel sauce, frying the sandwich, toasting the sandwich …

My thinking is that this is a simple dish and should therefore be simple to make. It's essentially a workers' lunch, so cooking a separate béchamel is probably out. Toasting, frying, grilling – it doesn't matter, as long as the result is crunchy and not soggy.

SERVES 4
8 slices good quality
    sandwich bread
8 slices ham
250 g (9 oz) grated gruyère
    cheese plus 8 slices
2 egg yolks
4 tablespoons thick
    (double/heavy) cream

Preheat the gill (broiler).

Toast 4 slices of the bread – these will be your sandwich bases. Top each toasted slice with a slice of ham, a slice of gruyère, then another slice of ham and another slice of gruyère.

Mix the grated cheese, egg yolks and cream in a bowl and season well. Spread half of this mixture on the 4 untoasted slices of bread and place these, cheese side down, on top of the bases. Spread the remaining cheese and egg mixture on the top of each sandwich. Place under the grill until golden brown and bubbling hot. Serve immediately.

238

# FRENCH ONION SOUP WITH CHEESY CROUTONS

There are some dishes that I could never get sick of and this is one of them. I could eat it every day. This soup is an exercise in balance and every time you make it will require a different touch, as onions change in their sweetness and acidity throughout the year.

SERVES 4

100 g (3½ oz) unsalted butter
4 large onions, thinly sliced
1 tablespoon plain (all-purpose) flour
3 thyme sprigs, leaves picked
1 fresh bay leaf
1 tablespoon sherry or cider vinegar
300 ml (10 fl oz) sweet cider
100 ml (3½ fl oz) dry white wine
600 ml (20½ fl oz) beef stock
50 ml (1¾ fl oz) brandy
8 baguette slices
1 garlic clove, halved
200 g (7 oz) hard, cooked curd cheese, grated (gruyère is traditional)

Melt the butter in a large saucepan or stockpot over medium heat. Add the onion and sauté, stirring regularly, until caramelised and golden brown. This will take around 60–90 minutes – be careful they don't burn or your soup will taste bitter. Stir in the flour, thyme and bay leaf and cook for a few more minutes before gradually adding the vinegar, cider, wine, stock and brandy. Bring to the boil, then reduce to a low simmer and cook for about 1 hour.

Meanwhile rub the baguette slices with the garlic clove halves.

Preheat the grill (broiler).

Remove the bay leaf from the soup and discard. To serve, ladle the soup into bowls and float a couple of baguette slices on top. Sprinkle a handful of cheese on top of the bread and place under the grill to melt the cheese.

Serve immediately.

# STRACCIATELLA

This is testament to the fact that the simplest things are often the best; a fact that Italian cooking has at its core. Don't you dare think about making this with commercially made chicken stock!

SERVES 4

1.5 litres (51 fl oz/3 cups) home-made chicken stock
4 eggs
120 g (4½ oz) finely grated aged cheese, think parmesan and grana styles
large handful flat-leaf parsley, finely chopped
pinch of freshly grated nutmeg

CHICKEN STOCK

1.5 kg (3 lbs 5 oz) chicken wings, rinsed
1 onion, unpeeled, sliced
1 large carrot, unpeeled, cut into 5 cm (2 in) pieces
1 celery stalk (with leaves), roughly chopped
6 mushrooms, thickly sliced
2 fresh bay leaves
1 thyme sprig
2 sprigs flat-leaf parsley
6 peppercorns

To make the stock, place the chicken wings in a large stockpot. Cover with 4 litres (135 fl oz/16 cups) water. Bring to the boil, uncovered, over medium heat, then immediately turn the heat down to a low simmer. Add the remaining ingredients and gently simmer, uncovered, for 3 hours. Set aside to cool. Cover and refrigerate overnight. Remove the fat from the stock surface using a spoon. There should be about 2 litres (68 fl oz/8 cups) of stock left – you will need 1.5 litres (51 fl oz/3 cups) for the soup, so freeze whatever is left over.

Bring the chicken stock to the boil in a large saucepan, then reduce the heat to a low simmer.

Whisk the eggs, cheese, parsley and nutmeg together in a bowl. Season generously with salt and pepper.

Remove the stock from the heat and allow it to sit for a minute until it becomes still. Pour in the egg mixture and leave for 30 seconds, to allow the egg to cook. Gently stir with a fork to break up the egg. (If you pour the egg into moving stock or if you stir it too soon, the soup will become grainy and cloudy – the egg should look more like little dumplings than fine strands.)

Serve immediately.

242

# BRUSSELS SPROUT SLAW WITH PECORINO

I have absolutely no time for people who do not like brussels sprouts. Normally, what they really mean is that they don't like the foul, grey versions from their childhood. Fair enough … change the way you cook them then! Or in this case, don't cook them at all. This slaw is really just a sneaky, healthy way to eat cheese anyway. Use a hard, tangy sheep's or goat's cheese to keep the flavours in this dish light and fresh. You could easily leave the bacon out if you wanted to be virtuous.

SERVES 6 AS A SIDE DISH

2 rashers (slices) bacon, rind removed, cut into 4 mm (¼ in) strips
500 g (1 lb 2 oz) brussels sprouts, trimmed
30 g (1 oz/¼ cup) slivered almonds, toasted
35 g (1¼ oz/¼ cup) hazelnuts, roasted and skins rubbed off with a tea towel
150 g (5½ oz) pecorino, shaved using a vegetable peeler

DRESSING

60 ml (2 fl oz/¼ cup) olive oil
1 tablespoon apple cider vinegar
1 tablespoon honey
1 tablespoon seeded mustard
zest of 1 lemon
1 tablespoon lemon juice
1 garlic clove, finely chopped
¼ teaspoon sea salt

Make the dressing by whisking all of the ingredients together in a bowl. Set aside.

Fry off the bacon until crisp, drain any excess fat and set aside to cool.

Use the shredding blade on a food processor (or some good knife skills) to finely shred the sprouts. Transfer to a large bowl and pour over the dressing. Add the bacon and nuts and mix thoroughly.

Transfer the dressed sprout slaw to a salad bowl and sprinkle with the cheese.

## INDUSTRIAL, ARTISANAL & FARMHOUSE CHEESE

The words industrial, artisanal and farmhouse are often used to label cheese.

### Industrial
To feed the world's growing population, our methods of food production have become more and more industrialised. This means giving preference to hyper-productive breeds, subjected to compromised standards of animal husbandry and health. Milk is usually heat-treated and standardised and commercial starter cultures are almost always used to make cheese. Milk processing is mechanised and traditional maturation is replaced with modern techniques that minimise weight loss and labour costs.

### Artisanal
This does not exclusively mean small, but producers of artisanal cheese do follow a series of choices to ensure the quality of the cheese. Artisan cheese is usually made with small herds, selected for their breed character rather than productivity, which graze on pastures of high species diversity. The milk is minimally treated and traditional techniques and equipment are used in cheese production.

### Farmhouse
This cheese is made on the same farm where the milk comes from. Depending on the size of the farm, it is usually an excellent indication of an artisanal approach to farming and production.

Rubbing wheels of Tom at Bruny Island
Cheese Co. helps distribute the mould
spores to encourage the development of
the rind on new cheeses.

# TWO-CHEESE AGNOLOTTI WITH SAGE BUTTER

I am a pretty lazy cook and the thought of making dozens of tiny ravioli by hand is pretty uninspiring. That's why I love agnolotti. They are big, fat pockets of stuffed pasta and you only need a few per person. The best bit is that you get lots of the cheesy stuffing and less of the pasta – the way it should be.

SERVES 4

100 g (3½ oz) unsalted butter
20 sage leaves

PASTA DOUGH

375 g (13 oz) pasta flour,
    sifted, plus extra for
    dusting
½ teaspoon salt
4 eggs, at room temperature

FILLING

150 g (5½ oz) fresh ricotta
    (see note)
80 g (2¾ oz) parmesan,
    grated (see note)
pinch of freshly grated
    nutmeg

> **NOTE** You can use any combination of cheese for this, and you don't need to limit yourself to just two varieties. The ricotta works as a good base because it is bulky and not strongly flavoured. You could use any fresh cheese as a substitute.

To make the pasta dough, tip the flour onto a clean work surface and form a mound. Sprinkle the salt over the flour and then form a well in the centre. Break the eggs into the well and use a fork to whisk them, incorporating some of the flour as you go. Keep doing this until you need to swap the fork for your fingers. Continue mixing until you have a ball of dough. If it is still a bit sticky, work in a bit more flour.

Knead well with your hands for at least 5 minutes. Really stretch it by holding the dough down with the palm of one hand and pushing it away from you with the heel of your other hand. Wrap in plastic wrap then set aside to rest.

To make the filling, mix the ricotta, parmesan and nutmeg in a bowl and season with salt and pepper. Set aside.

Divide the pasta into quarters and roll through a pasta machine until it is 1 mm (³⁄₆₄ in) thick. If you don't have a pasta machine, don't worry, it will be easy to roll thinly by hand, just keep it well floured.

Using a 10 cm (4 in) round biscuit (cookie) cutter, cut as many circles as possible. Re-roll the leftover dough to get a few more circles. Place a heaped teaspoon of the cheese mix to one side of each pasta circle. Use your finger to moisten the inside edge with water, then fold the circle over to create a half-moon shape. Gently squeeze the edge together to seal. Place the agnolotti on a floured baking tray.

Bring a large saucepan of salted water to the boil.

Melt the butter in a frying pan over medium heat. Add the sage leaves and cook until the butter starts to brown and the leaves become crisp. Remove from the heat but keep warm.

Cook the agnolotti in the boiling water until they float to the surface, about 2 minutes. Use a slotted spoon to lift them out and drain well before placing on plates. Pour the hot sage butter sauce over the top and serve immediately.

# FONDUE

I am on a personal quest to rid fondue of its daggy reputation and bring it back into the zeitgeist in all its deserving glory. One of my proudest moments on this quest came recently when I asked Wilkie, my seven-year-old son, what he wanted me to cook for his birthday dinner. You guessed it ... fondue. I am not sure if I felt more proud as a father, or as a cheesemaker.

Most people know fondue as the national dish of Switzerland. However, if you look up 'fondue' in the *Larousse Gastronomique*, the French dictionary of food and cooking, you will find that fondue is also a vegetable preparation that is cooked in butter or oil until it is reduced to a pulp. Forget about that. Let's stick to the cheese version.

The typical Swiss cheese fondue is the traditional Neuchâtel fondue, and in each canton of Switzerland there is a regional variation of the recipe. Fondues originally came into existence because of the geography and climate of Switzerland. In winter, when the mountains were covered with snow, cheesemakers in the Alpine chalets were cut off from villages for several months at a time, forcing them to rely on their own resources. The local produce of these mountain villages was mainly bread, cheese and wine. Fondue not only allowed these ingredients to be combined but it also provided an outlet for the cheese that was drying out as isolation progressed. It is also a very warming dish and perfect for the Alpine climate.

Fondues are cooked and served in a communal pot. The traditional pot is made of earthenware and is wide and shallow. In France and Switzerland it is called a 'caquelon'. Traditionally, fondue is served with stale bread. Each person spears a piece of bread on the end of their fork and swirls it in the fondue in a figure-of-eight fashion. If each person stirs as they dip the fondue will stay creamy until the end.

I always serve pickles and thinly sliced charcuterie with fondue, and a simple salad on the side. That way it is a bit more of a well-rounded meal and you don't end up feeling like you've just swallowed an anchor.

Oh, and don't even think about chocolate fondue. That's for people way less sophisticated than you.

## TIPS FOR MAKING THE PERFECT FONDUE

- An earthenware caquelon is definitely the best pot to use but a heavy cast-iron pot is also very good. Copper and stainless-steel pots may be used but the cheese will burn and stick to the pot far more quickly.
- Use the best, most mature cheese you can buy and grate it coarsely.
- Use a dry white wine, riesling or chardonnay. The wines of the French and Swiss mountains are generally white wines that are dry and heavily wooded and aged.
- The more acid there is in the wine the better the cheese will melt. If you are in doubt as to the acidity of the wine, add a squeeze of lemon juice.
- Make sure the wine is just starting to simmer before you add the cheese.
- Stir continuously in a figure-of-eight motion until the cheese is completely melted.
- Always keep the flame low – the cooking should be a slow, gradual process.
- If the fondue starts to curdle it can sometimes be saved with the addition of a few drops of lemon juice and some vigorous stirring.
- If your fondue is too thin, add some more cheese and melt this in and/or add some more cornflour (cornstarch) mixed with a little warmed wine.
- Use day-old bread – it will stay on your fork better.
- Bring the fondue to a simmer and allow to bubble gently – do not let it boil.

# FONDUE

SERVES 4
1 garlic clove
375 ml (12½ fl oz/1½ cups)
   dry white wine
1 teaspoon lemon juice
400 g (14 oz/4 cups) grated
   hard cheese, use at least
   two different varieties
3 tablespoons kirsch
1 tablespoon cornflour
   (cornstarch)
white pepper, to taste
freshly grated nutmeg,
   to taste
paprika, to taste
bread for dipping –
   baguettes are good

Light your fondue burner and put in place. Rub the inside of the fondue pot with the garlic clove and add the wine and lemon juice. Bring to a simmer and gradually add the cheese, stirring continuously in a figure-of-eight motion.

Combine the kirsch and cornflour in a bowl and, when the cheese mixture starts to bubble gently and all the cheese is completely melted, stir this in and cook for 2–3 minutes to thicken.

Season to taste with white pepper, nutmeg and paprika, and serve with chunks of bread for dipping.

# FORT DES ROUSSES

To watch Jean-Charles Arnaud walk down the rows of Comté in his incredible maturation facility, tapping and 'listening' to each cheese, is truly a memory I cherish.

Jean-Charles has 32 cheese producers, or 'fruitières' that supply him young cheeses made from the milk of Montbéliarde cows from approximately 400 farms. This symbiotic system has been in place in Jura for over 200 years. The responsibility for the quality of the cheese is understood and shared between the farmer, cheesemaker and affineur and the price paid to each party is dictated by the sale price of the cheese, further demonstrating the harmonious balance of the system. The young cheeses receive incredible amounts of attention, with the newly formed rounds kept in a special fermentation cellar, which enables the living organisms inside and outside the cheese to flourish. The bacteria inside increases up to 100,000 times in these ideal conditions over the first four months.

The final stages of the maturing process take place in a slow-maturing cellar and a storage cellar, where the rounds of cheese undergo most of their physical changes. I was especially fascinated to learn about the role of ammonia in these rooms and its effect on the texture of the cheese. Ammonia is commonly emitted by ageing cheese and is normally extracted from the maturation rooms as quickly as possible. Jean-Charles is convinced that it plays an import part in developing the desirable suppleness in Comté.

Jean-Charles has spent much of his life dedicated to this single cheese. His facility, high in the Jura mountains, is the extraordinary Fort des Rousses, which was built in 1862 to house over 3500 soldiers to help protect France from a Swiss invasion. Jean-Charles converted the fort to cheese cellars in 1997, which now house over 100,000 wheels of Comté in various stages of maturation. When I was last there, work was being carried out on a new, recently discovered section of the fort that will provide capacity for an additional 50,000 wheels of cheese.

Jean-Charles Arnaud taps on a wheel to listen for cracks.

**YOU HAVE BEEN A GUARDIAN OF ONE OF THE MOST IMPORTANT CHEESES IN FRANCE FOR MANY YEARS. HAS COMTÉ CHANGED DURING YOUR LIFETIME?**

*About 15 years ago, the Comté board decided to keep the raw milk temperature at 12°C (54°F). This was a very important decision because it helped to maintain the quality of the cheese.*

**AS SOMEONE WHO HAS BEEN RESPONSIBLE FOR THE MATURATION OF MILLIONS OF WHEELS OF COMTÉ, WHAT HAVE YOU LEARNED REGARDING THE AGEING PROCESS?**

*The maturing process for Comté cheese is very complex. Each wheel stays in a succession of cellars with different levels of temperature and humidity. The microflora growing on the surface of each wheel contributes to the total transformation of the texture of the cheese.*

**TO PRODUCE GREAT COMTÉ, WHAT DO YOU NEED TO CONTROL AND WHAT DO YOU LEAVE TO NATURAL PROCESSES?**

*It's compulsory to check the bacterial levels in the cheese, along with pH levels and temperature. But the quality of the pasture and the surrounding ecosystem in which the cows live is left to nature. This is just as essential to the final flavour of each wheel.*

**YOU ARE THE PRESIDENT OF INAO – THE FRENCH INSTITUTE FOR ORIGIN AND QUALITY, WHICH PRESCRIBES HOW AND WHERE TRADITIONAL CHEESES IN FRANCE CAN BE MADE. THESE REGULATIONS PRESERVE THE TRADITIONS OF FOOD IN EUROPE, BUT IS IT AT THE EXPENSE OF INNOVATION?**

*As the French President of INAO, it is my responsibility to write the laws and production rules for each PDO cheese. Of course we strive to preserve the traditional ways of production, but Comté has over 2000 years of history, so we have to bring some methods up to date. It's necessary to innovate, but we must do so in ways that preserve tradition and quality.*

# PROPER LASAGNE

Don't freak out, this is worth the effort. Like any traditional pasta dish, it should be the pasta that is the star of the show. If you can, make fresh pasta. If not, use a good quality dried egg pasta. Both are acceptable. I add cheese to my béchamel to give it a bit of extra richness. Maybe that's not entirely traditional but it feels right.

SERVES 6

fresh pasta sheets (see
    recipe below) or good
    quality dried egg lasagne
    sheets
100 g (3½ oz) Parmigiano
    Reggiano, grated

PASTA DOUGH

375 g (13 oz) pasta flour,
    sifted, plus extra for
    dusting
½ teaspoon salt
4 eggs, at room temperature

RAGÙ

2½ tablespoons olive oil
1 large onion, finely chopped
1 carrot, finely chopped
4 garlic cloves, finely
    chopped
500 g (1 lb 2 oz) gravy beef,
    finely chopped
500 g (1 lb 2 oz) minced
    (ground) pork
1 rosemary sprig, leaves
    picked and chopped
4 sage leaves, finely chopped
handful of flat-leaf parsley
    leaves, chopped
2 fresh bay leaves
200 g (7 oz) tomato paste
    (concentrated purée)
200 ml (7 fl oz) red wine
2 litres (68 fl oz/8 cups) beef
    stock

To make the pasta dough, tip the flour onto a clean work surface and form a mound. Sprinkle the salt over the flour and then form a well in the centre. Break the eggs into the well and use a fork to whisk them, incorporating some of the flour as you go. Keep doing this until you need to swap the fork for your fingers. Continue mixing until you have a ball of dough. If it is still a bit sticky, work in a bit more flour.

Knead the dough for at least 5 minutes. Really stretch it by holding the dough down with the palm of one hand and pushing it away from you with the heel of your other hand. Wrap in plastic wrap, then set aside to rest.

To make the ragù, heat the olive oil in a large heavy-based saucepan over medium heat. Add the onion, carrot and garlic and sauté for about 5 minutes. Add the beef and pork and stir for another 10 minutes until the meat starts to brown. Add the herbs and tomato paste and cook for a further 5 minutes. Pour in the wine and stock and bring to the boil. Reduce the heat to a low simmer and cook for about 1 hour, stirring occasionally, to prevent it from catching, until the sauce is thick and rich.

Divide the dough into quarters and roll by hand on a lightly floured work surface or through a pasta machine until it is 2–3 mm (⅛ in) thick. Cut into pieces about half the size of your baking dish.

Cook the lasagne sheets in salted boiling water for 2–3 minutes until almost al dente. Drain, and put into a bowl of cold water with a few drops of olive oil to prevent the sheets from sticking together.

If using dried pasta, cook in a large pan of salted boiling water with a couple of added drops of olive oil. Blanch, in batches to stop it clumping together, for 1 minute, then drain, separate and leave on an oiled tray or board. Set aside to cool. (See note on page 260.)

For the béchamel, put the milk, onion, bay leaf and clove in a saucepan and heat gently until simmering (do not let it boil). Remove from the heat and leave to stand for 15 minutes to allow the flavours to infuse.

*continues ...*

*continues ...*

## BÉCHAMEL

1 litre (34 fl oz/4 cups) full-cream (whole) milk
½ small onion, roughly chopped
1 fresh bay leaf
1 clove
100 g (3½ oz) butter
100 g (3½ oz) plain (all-purpose) flour
200 g (7 oz/2 cups) grated hard cheese such as Parmigiano Reggiano, pecorino or similar
200 g (7 oz) fresh ricotta
a little freshly grated nutmeg
white pepper

Make a roux by melting the butter in another heavy-based saucepan over medium heat. Add the flour and stir with a wooden spoon until the mixture forms a smooth paste. Cook, stirring constantly, for a couple of minutes. Remove from the heat.

Strain the warm milk into the roux and whisk together. Gradually bring to the boil, whisking vigorously to avoid any lumps, then reduce the heat to low and simmer for 10 minutes. Add the cheeses and nutmeg and stir until the cheese is melted and the sauce has a nice sheen. Season with salt and white pepper and set aside.

Preheat the oven to 180°C (350°F).

Ladle a small amount of ragù into a large baking dish and cover with a layer of lasagne sheets. Ladle more ragù over the sheets and spoon over some béchamel. Continue this layering process until you have used up all of the ingredients. Finish with a final layer of béchamel and sprinkle the grated Parmigiano Reggiano over the top. Bake for 30–40 minutes, or until cooked through and bubbling.

> **NOTE** Blanching dried pasta sheets first means they will not soak up moisture from the béchamel or ragù, which will keep your lasagne nice and saucy.

## HIGH-ALTITUDE CHEESES

Mountain cheeses have a special place in my heart. I love their inherent seasonality and the often simple technology used to make them. I have loved every moment of the large parts of my life spent making cheese in the mountains – the stunning vistas, the bracing fresh air and the sound of cow bells bouncing off the mountainsides. Ironically, I now make cheese on a beach at sea level.

Throughout the Alpine regions of France, Switzerland, Austria, Germany and Italy you will find some of the greatest cheeses on the planet. Because of their isolation, they have largely been quarantined from the industrialisation and bastardisation that has corrupted so many traditional cheeses in more accessible regions.

Mountain cheeses all tend to be large and long maturing because the cheesemakers spend summer and autumn on fresh mountain pastures and stay there until the snow returns. There is little point in making a cheese that needs to be sold and eaten within a few weeks when you are perched on a mountainside at 1800 metres (5900 feet), isolated from the rest of the cheese-eating world.

In the French and Swiss Alps, cheesemaking huts are called 'alpage', and alpage-made cheeses are highly sought after due to the complexity they gain from the richly varied mountain pastures. The explosion of native grasses, flowering perennials and herbs that grow in Alpine regions during the short snow-free seasons is a sight to behold and results in milk of incredible richness and flavour.

A typical alpage is often two or three floors high and will house the animals, people and the cheesemaking equipment. They usually rely on the burning of wood for heating the milk and cooking the curd (which is often done in copper vats shaped like a witch's cauldron). Animals graze the mountain pastures freely, usually without the confinement of fences or paddocks and the farmers and shepherds locate their herds by listening for the unique sounds of their bells. Because of the nature of Alpine farming and cheesemaking, herd sizes are small, usually less than 20 cows, which produce around 350 litres (92 gallons) of milk per day – enough to make only one or two wheels of gruyère.

# CHORLEY CAKES AND CHEDDAR CHEESE

Eccles cakes, those delectable, small, round cakes from Manchester made with flaky pastry, filled with currants and topped with sugar, are considered to be the thing to serve with cheddar. But I prefer their lesser-known country cousin from Lancashire. Chorley cakes are not as sweet, made with shortcrust pastry and are flatter, like a biscuit (cookie). I add a bit of apple to mine but you can leave it out if you want to stick with the original recipe.

MAKES 10

1 granny smith apple, peeled, cored and grated
100 g (3½ oz) currants
½ teaspoon freshly grated nutmeg
50 g (1¾ oz) soft brown sugar
350 g (12½ oz) plain (all-purpose) flour, plus extra for dusting
180 g (6½ oz) chilled unsalted butter, cut into small cubes
zest of 1 orange
25 ml (¾ fl oz) full-cream (whole) milk
cheddar cheese, to serve

Preheat the oven to 200°C (400°F). Line a baking tray with baking paper.

Mix the apple, currants, nutmeg and sugar in a bowl and set aside.

Place the flour and butter in a large bowl and use your fingertips to rub the butter through the flour until it resembles fine breadcrumbs.

Make a well in the flour mixture and add 75 ml (2½ fl oz) water and the orange zest. Use a wooden spoon to mix together to form a dough. Turn the mixture out onto a lightly floured work surface and knead for a couple of minutes until the dough is smooth. Roll out to form a slab about 4–5 mm (¼ in) thick. Divide into 10 even squares. Place a teaspoon of the apple and currant mixture in the centre of each square and bring the edges together to form a sealed pocket. Use your fingers to pinch the pastry edges together. Turn the pockets over and lightly roll to flatten them a bit. You want the finished cakes to be about 8–10 mm (⅓ in) thick. Poke a small hole in the top of each pocket to let the steam escape.

Transfer the cakes to the baking tray and brush with the milk. Bake in the oven for about 25 minutes or until golden brown. Allow to cool, then serve with wedges of good quality, aged cheddar.

262

# SELECTING AND SERVING CHEESE

There are shops that sell cheese and then there are cheesemongers. Knowing a good cheesemonger is as important as knowing a good accountant, but a cheesemonger will make your life way more pleasurable.

### How to spot a great cheesemonger

The best approach to finding a great cheese supplier is to start with the basic premise to eliminate as many links from the supply chain as possible. The cheese on the shelf at your local shop may have gone through the hands of several importers, distributors, shipping agents and wholesale companies before it gets to you. The alternative to this global industrialised system is to buy cheese directly from the cheesemaker. This way, not only will you be supporting and consuming local produce, you will also be receiving cheese that is at its seasonal best.

Farmers' markets and farm-gate stores are often the best places to buy cheese. It puts you directly in contact with the folk that made it and gives you a fuller understanding of the stories behind each cheese. Many cheesemakers will now also send their cheeses directly to your home. Having an ongoing relationship with the people that make your cheese is a terrific thing! Whoever you buy your cheese from, take their cheeses as you find them. It is a moving target – the cheese you bought last month will almost certainly be different this month. Make sure you taste it first and ask questions about how it was made and how it was aged. Good cheese can be expensive, and for the dedicated it is possible to spend considerable money over the course of a year, so make sure you are getting good value. Once you have established a good relationship with a cheesemonger, trust them, take their advice, learn from them but also share your experiences and preferences with them.

### Choosing your cheese

Engage your senses when buying cheese. Cheese has aroma, texture, flavour and form. First, does it look like it should? If the cut surface looks dry, sweaty or oily, reject it. Does it smell fresh, natural and delicious? Are there any off smells or too much ammonia? Does it even smell at all? Does it feel like it should? Is it soft or hard? Supple or crumbly?

### Looking after your cheese at home

It is fair to say that almost no cheese will be made better by storing it at your house. The best situation is

266

Formaggio Kitchen, Cambridge, Massachusetts.

to buy small amounts of cheese, often. Store it in your belly, I say! Once a cheese has been cut, the clock is ticking. A cut wedge of cheese is open to the elements and can be adversely affected by air, temperature, bacteria and moulds and poor wrapping. So don't be overly enthusiastic when buying cheese because the cheesemaker or cheesemonger you are buying it from will be much better equipped to store cheese than you (mainly because they are storing whole wheels).

So, what is the best way to store cheese at home? Most artisan cheese is happiest in a damp cellar, which is unfortunately, for most people, hard to come by nowadays. The best solution is to try and achieve cellar-like conditions to store larger quantities of cheese. I have seen some of my customers use garages, spare rooms, car boots, shoe boxes, laundries ... You

might need to get creative to find the right place! But in the end, most people just use their fridge, which is fine as long as you prevent the cheese from drying out and let the cheese warm to room temperature before you serve it.

For small amounts of cheese, try having a dedicated plastic container with a lid. You can use this for storing a few different cheeses, just make sure they are wrapped separately so the flavours and aromas do not get cross-contaminated. An airtight container will stop the cheese from drying out (the inside of your fridge can be a pretty drying environment when the door is closed, that's why the celery always looks limp!) and will also help to increase the humidity, especially if there are a couple of soft cheeses in the box.

## Temperature

At home, most cheeses are best kept between 10°C–14°C (50°F–57°F), as this is the temperature range they are matured at. Any warmer than this and the cheese will sweat, ooze oil from the cut surface, feel pappy and smell stronger than usual. The visual warnings for cheese stored too cold are less obvious, but it will taste and smell bland and feel inert. In the interests of flavour, you are almost always better erring on the warmer side for cheese storage – this might mean buying smaller pieces and storing them for less time.

If you want to slow down the ripening process in order to keep the cheese longer, wrap it well and store in a cool place (ideally not less than 5°C/40°F); however, don't forget to return it to room temperature before eating to allow the flavours to revive.

## Humidity

Humidity is even more important than temperature. Most cheeses should be kept at a relative humidity of 80% or more; however, most people don't have a hygrometer at home, so here are the signs to look out for:
● If the cut surface of your cheese grows a thick layer of mould then the atmosphere is too wet. A light

*Milk. Made.*

bloom, like the fuzz on a peach, on a cut surface, however, is a sign that the atmosphere is nice and humid. Just scrape or cut it off. Mould on cheese is perfectly normal and natural. In fact it is often an indication that you are storing your cheese properly. Throwing out good cheese because it has mould on it is moronic. Mould should not be feared!

- If cracking occurs, then the atmosphere is too dry. Cracked, dried-out cheese is difficult to rescue. If it has not gone too far, try covering it with a damp cloth.

## Wrapping

Real cheeses are living, breathing things. Wrapping cheese in plastic wrap will cause it to become soggy, sweaty and smelly. Imagine what would happen if I wrapped you in plastic wrap and left you for a week or so! But left uncovered, cheese will dry out. Your cheesemonger should use special breathable paper that achieves a balance between these two extremes; keep your cheese wrapped in this paper even after you have opened it. An alternative is waxed paper – the sort used to wrap sandwiches. You can also use a plastic zip-lock bag for a few days; just make sure you leave plenty of air in the bag.

## Creating the perfect cheese platter

For me, there are two options:

**The knockout blow:** This is my preferred option; the less is more approach. A single, awesome cheese that is the result of a very thoughtful choice. A cheese in perfect condition and one that is visually wonderful, texturally sublime and delivers incredible flavour. A cheese so good that putting anything else on the board would detract from it.

Here are a couple of examples to give you the idea:
- Cloth-matured cheddar with Chorley Cakes (see page 262) and stout.
- A strong blue cheese with Rye and Molasses Biscuits (see page 274) and vintage port.
- A pungent washed rind with sourdough bread and cider.

**The multiple-choice statement:** In some instances, it is more ideal to serve several cheeses together. If this is the case, then your number one rule is BALANCE. To achieve this, you will need more than two cheeses but less than five. Balance means finding a diversity of styles, age profiles, flavours, textures and milks. What you don't want is three cheeses that are too similar. A soft goat's cheese, a sheep's milk blue and a hard cow's milk cheese is a great mix, for example.

Regardless of which path you venture down, make sure your cheese is completely at room temperature before serving. I prefer to serve cheese on a simple wooden board because it is a natural product and a plain background which lets the cheese stand out. A slate or terracotta tile is also a good option.

## How to cut your cheese

Another thing I am rather fussy about is knives. Make sure you provide a knife for each cheese so that you don't get bits of your blue cheese mixed in with your subtle goat's cheese.

The rule is that when you are cutting some cheese for yourself, take your fair share of the rind with you. Don't just dig in to the middle with no respect for either the cheese or your fellow cheese eaters. If it is a round of cheese then cut a wedge from the middle, mimicking the spokes of a wheel. If it is a wedge of cheese, cut a slice from the side, taking some of the rind with you.

## Bread or crackers?

Perhaps the question you should really ask is do you need anything at all? Personally, I like to taste the cheese and enjoy its texture without anything else. Hard cheeses can be sliced and eaten with fingers, allowing you to fully appreciate their flavour and texture. Some people – more delicate than myself – prefer to use bread or crackers for their soft cheeses to keep their fingers clean. Each to their own.

If you are going to serve crackers or bread with your cheese, there are a couple of directions you can take.

One of Paris's finest cheese shops, in the 7th arrondissement.

or membrillos because the acid is tempered and you can control the level of sweetness. Autumn fruits like apples, pears, figs and quinces seem to work better than summer berries or tropical fruit. On Bruny Island we spice cherries from a local orchard and they are terrific with most cheeses.

Always choose an accompaniment that will complement the flavour of the cheese rather than compete with it. Sugar will balance salty (think classics such as Gorgonzola drizzled with honey or an aged cheddar served with dense fruit cake) and acid will complement acid (a young, tart goat's cheese with slices of crisp, fresh pear, for example).

You can go for something neutral in flavour so that the cheese shines through; or you can try and complement your cheese with a flavoured bread or cracker.

## Cheese accompaniments

As I've already said, a good cheese itself does not need anything to make it better, but sometimes a well considered accompaniment can enrich the whole experience of enjoying cheese. Generally, other than a beautiful crisp apple or pear, fresh fruit is rarely the best option as the natural acid in fruit can be a bit unfriendly to cheese. I love the flavours that arise from cooked fruit, in the form of compotes, jellies, jams

**You are going to want something to drink ...**

**Red wine**: I need to get something off my chest. Red wine and cheese are not natural partners. I know that is going to be hard for some to get their heads around (especially some of my winemaking mates), but there, I've said it.

With wine you are dealing with elements such as tannins, astringency, acidity, wood and often high amounts of alcohol; in cheese you are dealing with some pretty robust flavours as well, including fats, salt, moulds and bacteria. Granted, there can be some sublime experiences to be had with wine and cheese together but this is far from an automatic outcome. Unfortunately, especially in countries like Australia, the tendency is to assume the perfect wine for any cheese is a 'big bottle of red' such as a shiraz or cabernet. This is wrong. Totally wrong! If anything, lighter styles of red, often from cooler climates where subtler wines that are more food-friendly are produced, will yield a better match. Tannins and astringency are public enemy number one to most cheeses, so wines with softer structures or those that have been bottle aged will nearly always work better.

**White wine**: Getting warmer ... Because white wines tend to have less aggressive tannins and astringency and are usually lower in alcohol, they are generally more appropriate cheese matches. Acidity is often the problem though – many white grape varieties possess acids so green and fresh that you involuntarily clench your butt cheeks when you drink them. That's fine with a new-born goat's cheese but horrible with a cheese that has any developed characteristics. Again, rounder styles, possibly with some oak and/or bottle age, are the better way to go.

**Bubbles:** I love Champagne (or, more correctly, sparkling wine in Australia) and have had some knee-trembling experiences matching vintage fizz with aged cheeses. Young, fresh cheeses also love sparkling wines. There is a whole wonderful world here for you to explore and I bid you a good journey.

**Cider:** Cheese and cider have had a long and fruitful friendship. The French region of Normandy is not only home to such benchmark cheeses such as camembert, Pont-l'Évêque and Livarot but it is also the spiritual home of cider – and it is no coincidence that strong, soft surface-ripened cheeses such as these work a treat with cider. English cheddar and Somerset cider is another classic combination. Where I live in Tasmania, there is a long history of cider-making that is currently having a revival, and the number of exceptionally good ciders is a boon for local cheese lovers.

**Beer:** Now we're talking. If there was ever an all-round, go-to drink that both complements and contrasts with cheese, it is beer. Of course, beer, like wine, is a many-varied thing and the gamut of flavours runs from sweet and fruity to bitter and savoury. It seems the world has rediscovered the joys of beer and the explosion of awesome beer producers in just about every Western country spells great news for cheese lovers. Lager is the least successful style, when compared with more structured and flavourful ales, porters and stouts (not to mention all the beers that don't fit neatly into these pigeonholes and fall between the cracks). Think cloth-matured cheddar with a rich, savoury stout or a meaty washed rind with fruity, hoppy ale.

**Whisky:** Definitely worth a mention if only because of the number of extremely enjoyable evenings I have had with a few mates, a bottle of single malt and a board of cheese. The robust savouriness of whisky pairs beautifully with big, aged cheeses or funky washed rinds in a way that often surprises. Peat-heavy malts can be a bit tricky but having said that, when matched with a smoked cheese, the result can leave you giddy with happiness.

Mary Holbrook, of Sleight Farm, near Bath, gave up being a historian to make cheese. Her goat's cheeses are some of the best in the UK.

# OATCAKES

The Scots have been eating oatcakes since before the Romans turned up. They should not be confused with bannocks, which are similar in Scotland at least, and cooked on a griddle. Oatcakes are the perfect partner for strong cheddar.

MAKES ABOUT 24

200 g (7 oz) fine or medium ground oats, plus extra for dusting
120 g (4½ oz) salted butter, diced
30 g (1 oz) rolled (porridge) oats
1 egg yolk
plain (all-purpose) flour, for dusting

Preheat the oven to 180°C (350°F). Line a baking tray with silicone paper.

In a large bowl, mix together the oatmeal, butter and oats, using your fingertips to rub the butter through until it has all gone. Add the egg yolk and mix with a wooden spoon – the dough should be pretty sticky. Season with salt.

Dust a clean work surface with half plain flour and half oatmeal. Roll the dough out until it is about 7–8 mm (⅓ in) thick. Using a 5 cm (2 in) biscuit (cookie) cutter, cut out as many rounds as possible. Roll out the leftover bits of dough and repeat until it is all used. Lift the rounds onto the baking tray and bake for about 15–20 minutes or until the biscuit edges turn golden brown.

Transfer to a wire rack to cool completely before serving or store in an airtight container for up to 10 days.

# RYE AND MOLASSES BISCUITS

When I was a kid I would spend my holidays on my auntie's dairy farm. I would stand in the dairy as the cows came in, gawking at the enormous black and white animals as they took their place on either side of the herringbone-arranged milking parlour. My uncle would pull on a rope to activate this great contraption and the cows would be locked in place. Their heads would go straight to the long metal trough in front of them where, with the pull of another rope, a mixture of grain and chaff would drop out. My job was to pour a line of molasses along the trough, which would be licked and slobbered on immediately by the greedy cows. These biscuits (cookies), made with rolled (porridge) oats and molasses, and great with blue cheese, will disappear just as fast.

MAKES ABOUT 30

120 g (4½ oz) unsalted butter, softened
200 g (7 oz) caster (superfine) sugar
1 egg
1 egg yolk
110 g (4 oz) molasses
1 tablespoon white vinegar
150 g (5½ oz/1 cup) plain (all-purpose) flour
150 g (5½ oz/1 cup) rye flour
50 g (1¾ oz) rolled (porridge) oats
1½ teaspoons bicarbonate of soda (baking soda)
1½ teaspoons salt
1 teaspoon fennel seeds
¼ teaspoon ground ginger

Preheat the oven to 180°C (350°F). Beat the butter and sugar in a bowl with a hand-held electric mixer for a few minutes until creamy. Beat in the egg and egg yolk and then the molasses and vinegar.

Stir in the remaining ingredients and combine well to form a soft dough. Take a tablespoon of dough at a time and roll into balls. Place the balls 5 cm (2 in) apart on a baking tray lined with baking paper. Flatten each ball slightly with the palm of your hand. Bake for 15–20 minutes until golden brown.

Cool on a wire rack completely before serving, or store in airtight container for up to 4 days.

# SALT AND PEPPER LAVOSH

Lavosh is a dry, unleavened bread from the Middle East, more akin to a biscuit (cracker) than a bread. You can add seeds or dried herbs to the dough to give it more character, but I love the neutral, simple flavour that a touch of salt and pepper adds. If you don't want your forearms to ache, you can roll the dough out through a pasta machine. These crispbreads are especially great with fresh and soft cheeses.

MAKES 30–35 PIECES

150 g (5½ oz/1 cup) plain (all-purpose) flour, plus extra for dusting
50 g (1¾ oz/⅓ cup) wholemeal (whole-wheat) flour
1½ teaspoons salt
1 teaspoon cracked black pepper
60 ml (2 fl oz/¼ cup) extra-virgin olive oil

Preheat the oven to 170°C (340°F).

Mix the flours, salt and pepper in a large mixing bowl. Make a well in the centre and pour in the oil and 125 ml (4 fl oz/½ cup) water. Mix well until you have a soft, pliable dough.

On a lightly floured work surface, roll out one quarter of the dough at a time until it is 1–2 mm (1/16 in) thick. Alternatively, roll the dough through a pasta machine. Cut the dough into 5 cm x 15 cm (2 in x 6 in) strips and carefully place on baking trays lined with baking paper.

Bake for about 15 minutes or until golden brown. Cool completely on a wire rack before storing in an airtight container for up to 2 weeks.

# WATER CRACKERS

These used to be called 'hardtack' and were a staple onboard ships undertaking long voyages at sea, where the only thing that would go the distance were these hard, dry biscuits made without shortening. Now we have conquered the planet, I reckon we can add a touch of olive oil without fear of ruin. Because these biscuits are pretty neutral in flavour, they are a great match for soft cheeses.

MAKES ABOUT 50

450 g (1 lb/3 cups) plain (all-purpose) flour, plus extra for dusting
1 teaspoon caster (superfine) sugar
2 teaspoons sea salt
4 tablespoons extra-virgin olive oil

Preheat the oven to 170°C (340°F).

Mix together the flour, sugar and salt in a large mixing bowl. Add the oil and 250 ml (8½ fl oz/1 cup) water and mix thoroughly until it forms a stiff dough (add a touch more water or flour if needed to achieve the desired consistency). Knead the dough for a few minutes on a lightly floured work surface until smooth. Divide the dough into three portions.

On a well floured work surface, roll the dough balls out to a thickness of 3–4 mm (⅛ in). (Depending on the gluten content of your flour, the dough may resist being rolled so thin and start to shrink back – if this happens, leave it to rest for 5–10 minutes while you have a cup of tea, then roll out again. Use a sharp knife or pizza cutter to cut into pieces – they can be whatever size or shape you like.

Place the crackers on a baking tray lined with baking paper (you can put them as close together as you like) and bake for 10–15 minutes, or until they are golden brown.

Cool on a wire rack completely before serving or storing in an airtight container for up to 2 weeks.

278

# RESOURCES

**For cheesemaking kits and merchandise visit:**
www.milkmadebook.com

## ASSOCIATIONS

**American Cheese Society**
www.cheesesociety.org
Good resource for courses, equipment
and employment.

**Specialist Cheesemakers Association**
www.specialistcheesemakers.co.uk

**Australian Specialist Cheesemakers'
Association**
www.australiancheese.org

## INFORMATION AND COURSES

**University of Guelph (CAN)**
www.uoguelph.ca/foodscience/
Great technical information on cheesemaking.

**Peter Dixon Cheesemaking Consulting (US)**
www.dairyfoodsconsulting.com

**Artisan Cheesemaking Academy (AUS)**
www.tafesa.edu.au/artisan-cheese-making-
academy-australia

**The School of Artisan Food (UK)**
www.schoolofartisanfood.org

**Bobolink Dairy (US)**
www.cowsoutside.com

## CULTURES AND CHEESEMAKING EQUIPMENT

**Fromagex**
www.fromagex.com

**Cultures Alive (AUS)**
www.culturesalive.com.au

**New England Cheesemaking Supply Co. (US)**
www.cheesemaking.com

**The Cheesemaker (US)**
www.thecheesemaker.com

**Cheeselinks (AUS)**
www.cheeselinks.com.au

**Home Make It (AUS)**
www.homemakeit.com.au

**Moorlands Cheesemakers (UK)**
www.cheesemaking.co.uk

**The Cheese Making Shop (UK)**
www.cheesemakingshop.co.uk

# FURTHER READING

Over the years I have put together a pretty sizeable library of cheese books. Here are some of the titles that I turn to and can recommend.

Androuet, P 1983, *Guide du Fromage*,
Aidan Ellis Publishing

Conley, S & Smith, P 2013, *Cowgirl Creamery Cooks*,
Chronicle

Davies, S 2012, *The Cheesemaker's Apprentice*,
Quarry Books

Donnelly, C (ed.) 2014, *Cheese and Microbes*,
ASM Press

Dubach, J 1983, *A Lifetime of Cheesemaking in Developing Countries*, SKAT Press

Dubach, J 1989, *Traditional Cheesemaking*,
ITDG Publishing

Evans, M, Haddow, N & O'Meara, R 2012,
*The Gourmet Farmer Deli Book*, Murdoch Books

Freeman, S 2003, *The Real Cheese Companion*,
Sphere Publishing

Herbst, ST & Herbst, R 2007, *The Cheese Lover's Companion*, William Morrow

Irvine, S 1998, *Mozzarella*,
Scriptum Editions

Janier, C 2014, *Le Fromage*,
Stéphane Bachès

Katz, SE 2012, *The Art of Fermentation*,
Chelsea Green Publishing

Kazuko, M 2005, *French Cheese*,
Eyewitness Companions, DK Publishing

Kindstedt, P 2005, *American Farmstead Cheese*,
Chelsea Green Publishing

Kindstedt, PS 2012, *Cheese and Culture*,
Chelsea Green Publishing

Le Jaouen, J-C 1990, *The Fabrication of Farmstead Goat Cheese*, Cheesemakers' Journal

Mendelson, A 2008, *Milk*,
Knopf

Rance, P 1989, *The French Cheese Book*,
Pan Macmillan

Rance, P 1988, *The Great British Cheese Book*,
Pan Macmillan

Raveneau, A 2014, *Vaches: Made in France*,
Rustica Editions

Schmid, R 2009, *The Untold Story of Milk*,
Newtrends Publishing

Scott, R 1998, *Cheesemaking Practice*,
Springer

Studd, W 1999, *Chalk and Cheese*,
Purple Egg

Thorpe, L 2009, *The Cheese Chronicles*,
Ecco Press

# ACKNOWLEDGEMENTS

Among the many people who made this book possible, I want to especially acknowledge the unwavering commitment and huge contribution from Alan Benson. This book is largely a result of his great generosity of spirit and inability to compromise. His indefatigable energy while chasing cheese around the globe, and his organisational skills when it came to planes, trains and automobiles were invaluable. Oh, and he also took the photos. Pretty nice, huh?

I am in debt to Jane Willson, my publisher at Hardie Grant. Thank you for your instant enthusiasm for this book and for making it happen; I hope you are proud of what we have created. I am also grateful to Jane's team at Hardie Grant for their guidance and support: project editor Meelee Soorkia, design manager Mark Campbell, editor Lucy Heaver, designer David Eldridge and design assistant Andy Warren.

To food stylists Michelle Crawford and Rhianne Contreras – thank you for making the food look great, and a huge rap to Claire Pietersen, who managed the cooking for the studio shoot.

Big thanks to all the farmers, cheesemakers, affineurs and cheesemongers along the way. You taught me, entertained me, fed me and inspired me.

To my incredible crew at Bruny Island Cheese Co. – especially my partners – who continually allow me the time to do things like write books while holding it all together in my absence.

And finally, to my wonderful partner Leonie – I could not hope for a more generous and supportive partner, and to our awesome kids, Tilla and Wilkie … thank you x.

282

# INDEX

**A**

agnolotti, Two-cheese agnolotti with sage butter 248
Aligot 212
animal rennet 106
apples
    Blue cheese, apple and leek pithivier 188
    Chorley cakes and cheddar cheese 262
Arancini 120
artisanal cheeses 246

**B**

bacon
    Brussels sprout slaw with pecorino 244
    Egg, bacon and cheddar pies 214
    Tartiflette 170
bacteria
    starter cultures 105, 110
    washed-rind cheeses 158
Baked onions in brie custard 166
Beaufort AOC 230–1
béchamel, Proper lasagne 258–260
beef
    Blue cheese steak sangers 190
    Cheesy polenta with meatballs 168
    Shish barak 82
beer, with cheese 270
beetroot, Roast beetroot and feta tart 128
benchmark blue cheeses 182–3
benchmark cooked curd cheeses 230–1
benchmark fresh cheeses 114–15
benchmark mould-ripened cheeses 157–8
benchmark semi-hard cheeses 204–5
benchmark washed-rind cheeses 159
Bengali yoghurt fish curry 84
Best-ever cheese biscuits 222
Billy cheese 46, 47
biscuits
    Best-ever cheese biscuits 222
    Butter shortbread 70
    Oatcakes 272
    Rye and molasses biscuits 268, 274
    Water crackers 278
    *see also* bread; snacks
blue cheese recipes
    Blue cheese, apple and leek pithivier 188

Blue cheese mayo 190
Blue cheese soufflés with pickled cherry and hazelnut salad 194
Blue cheese steak sangers 190
Blue cheese straws 186
Blue cheese and sweet onion pizza 198
Pear, walnut and blue cheese salad with honey dressing 192
blue cheeses 182–98, 274
    benchmark 182–3
bread
    Salt and pepper lavosh 276
    Whey and soured cream bread 148
    with cheese 268–9
breeds of dairy animals 24, 38–40, 98–9, 150, 176–7
brie 156
    Baked onions in brie custard 166
    difference from camembert 165
    Fig, brie and rosemary tart 172
    Brie de Coulommiers 158
    Brie de Meaux AOC 157–8
    Brie de Melun 158
    Brie de Nangis 158
Bruny Island Cheese Co. 10–11
Brussels sprout slaw with pecorino 244
buffalo milk 23
buffalo milk cheeses 22, 23, 115
burrata 114
butter 52–70
    composition 52
    making cultured butter 54
    types of 52–3
butter recipes
    Brown butter ice cream 62
    Butter shortbread 70
    Café de Paris butter 56
    Croissants 64–5
    Passionfruit butter 68
    Simple lemon butter sauce for seafood 58
buttermilk 53
Buttermilk fried chicken 60
Buttermilk scones 68

**C**

Cabécou de Rocamadour AOC 158
cacik 86
Café de Paris butter 56
camembert 156
    difference from brie 165
    Camembert de Normandie AOC 157

Cantal AOC 142, 205, 212, 218
casein 21
cattle breeds 24, 38, 98–9, 176, 177, 204, 254
cauliflower, Cauliflower cheese 220
Chabichou du Poitou 22, 158
cheddar 20, 177, 204, 210, 224–5, 272
    Best-ever cheese biscuits 222
    Chorley cakes and cheddar cheese 262
    Egg, bacon and cheddar pies 214
cheese accompaniments 268–9
cheese cave 98–9, 110
Cheese fricos 234
cheese platters 268
cheesemakers 16, 46–7, 98–9, 150–1, 200–1, 224–5, 254–5
cheesemaking 11, 20–1, 104–9, 261
    at home 109–11
    coagulation 105–6
    cutting, stirring and heating curds 106
    draining and hooping 106
    fermentation 105
    maturation 109, 110, 209
    natural cheesemaking 142
    preparation of the milk 104
    salting 106, 109
    *see also* specific types, e.g. ricotta
cheesemongers 266
cheeses
    and wood 218
    blue cheeses 182–98
    choosing and looking after at home 266–8
    cutting 268
    fresh cheeses 111, 114–42
    hard, cooked curd cheeses 230–61
    high altitude cheeses 261
    industrial, artisanal and farmhouse cheeses 246
    selecting and serving 266–78
    semi-hard cheeses 204–22
    surface-ripened cheeses 156–74
    wrapping 268
    *see also* specific types, e.g. brie
Cheesy polenta with meatballs 168
cherries
    Blue cheese soufflés with pickled cherry and hazelnut salad 194
    Cherry clafoutis 42
chicken
    Buttermilk fried chicken 60
    Chicken stock 242
    Yoghurt-marinated barbecue chicken 90

Yoghurt soup with chicken and
  rice 80
choosing cheese 266
Chorley cakes and cheddar cheese
  262, 268
cider, with cheese 270
clafoutis, cherry 42
clarified butter 53
coagulation 105–6
Colston Basset Stilton 135
Comté AOC 134, 231, 254–5
cooked curd cheese recipes
  see hard, cooked curd cheese
  recipes
cooked curd cheeses 230–61
  benchmark 230–1
cow breeds 24, 38, 98–9, 176–7, 204, 254
cow's milk 20, 22, 52, 75
cow's milk cheeses 106, 159, 165, 204,
  205, 230–1, 254
crackers, with cheese 268–9
crème fraîche
  Lemon crème fraîche ice cream 44
  making 24
Croissants 64–5
Croque monsieur 238
Crottin de Chavignol 22, 158
cultured butter 52–3
  making 54
curds 20, 105–6
Cured ocean trout, grapefruit and
  goat's curd 130
cutting cheese 268

D
dairy farms/dairy farmers 16, 24,
  46–7, 98–9, 150–1, 176–7, 224–5
desserts
  Brown butter ice cream 62
  Cherry clafoutis 42
  Honey, lemon and cardamom
    frozen yoghurt 92
  Honey, whisky and saffron
    cheesecake 138
  Icelandic skyr, honey and
    cinnamon cake 96
  Lemon crème fraîche ice cream 44
  Shrikhand 94
  South American buttermilk
    doughnuts filled with
    dulce de leche 36–7
dressings and mayonnaise 244
  Blue cheese mayo 190
  Honey walnut dressing 192

drinks
  Whey hot toddy 146
  with cheese 270
dulce de leche 36
Dutch Knuckle 99

E
Egg, bacon and cheddar pies 214
Emmentaler 230
enzymes 21
Époisses de Bourgogne AOC 159

F
farmhouse cheeses 246
fat 21–2
fermentation
  cheese 105, 134
  yoghurt 74
feta 114–15
  making 118–19
  Roast beetroot and feta tart 128
Fig, brie and rosemary tart 172
fior di latte 114
fish
  Bengali yoghurt fish curry 84
  Cured ocean trout, grapefruit and
    goat's curd 130
  Simple lemon butter sauce for
    seafood 58
flavour, raw milk cheese 134–5
fondue 250
  recipe 252
  tips for making 250
Fontina 168
food safety
  cheesemaking 109–10
  natural cheesemaking 142
  raw milk cheese 132–4
Fort des Rousses Comté 231, 254–5
Fort des Rousses, Haute-Savoie,
  France 254–5
Fort St. Antoine Comté 231
fresh cheese recipes
  Arancini 120
  Cured ocean trout, grapefruit and
    goat's curd 130
  The definitive margherita pizza
    136
  Mozzarella in carozza 124
  Ricotta gnudi with buttery peas 126
  Roast beetroot and feta tart 128
  Ross's ricotta shortcake 140
fresh cheeses 114–15
  benchmark fresh cheeses 114–15

making feta 118–19
  making fromage blanc 111
  making ricotta and paneer 116
fromage blanc, making 111
Fromage fort 236
fruit, with cheese 269

G
Garrotxa 22
ghee 53
gnudi 126
goat breeds 40, 46
goat's curd, Cured ocean trout,
  grapefruit and goat's curd 130
goat's milk 22–3, 52, 142
goat's milk cheeses 22, 46–7, 114, 156,
  158, 205
Gorgonzola Piccante 183
Gouda 231
grapefuit, Cured ocean trout, grapefruit
  and goat's curd 130
gruyère 230, 261
  Croque monsieur 238
  French onion soup with cheesy
    croutons 240

H
hard, cooked curd cheese recipes
  Brussels sprout slaw with pecorino 244
  Cheese fricos 234
  Croque monsieur 238
  Fondue 252
  French onion soup with cheesy
    croutons 240
  Proper lasagne 258–60
  Stracciatella 242
hard, cooked curd cheeses 230–61
  benchmark 230–1
high altitude cheeses 261
honey
  Honey, lemon and cardamom frozen
    yoghurt 92
  Honey walnut dressing 192
  Honey, whisky and saffron
    cheesecake 138
humidity
  in cheese maturation 209
  keeping cheeses at home 267–8
hygiene, cheesemaking 109–10

I
ice cream
  Brown butter ice cream 62
  Lemon crème fraîche ice cream 44

285

Icelandic skyr, honey and cinnamon cake 96
industrial cheeses 246
integrity of cheese 135

K
kefir 74
kofta, Wallaby kofta with cacik 86

L
La Sapalet, Switzerland 150–1
Labneh 76, 78
lactic coagulation 105, 114
lactose 21
Laguiole 205, 212
Lamb kofta with cacik 86
Lancashire cheese 210
Lasagne 258–60
leeks, Blue cheese, apple and leek pithivier 188
Lemon crème fraîche ice cream 44
Linguine with mushrooms and stinky cheese 174
Livarot 159, 270

M
Macaroni cheese 216
Manchego PDO 22, 38, 204–5
Maroilles 159
mascarpone, Honey, whisky and saffron cheesecake 138
maturation (cheese) 109, 110, 209
microbial rennet 106
milk 16–17
    characteristics 20
    composition 20–1
    factors affecting quality 16, 20
    from different animals 22–3
    products from 16
milk recipes
    Cherry clafoutis 42
    Lemon crème fraîche ice cream 44
    Milk puddings with elderflower caramel 30
    Pork loin braised in milk 26
    South American buttermilk doughnuts filled with dulce de leche 36–7
    Spanish fried milk 34
minerals 21
mould-ripened cheese recipes
    Baked onions in brie custard 166
    Fig, brie and rosemary tart 172

mould-ripened cheeses 156–8
    benchmark 157–8
    difference between brie and camembert 165
    making white mould cheese 160–3
    see also blue cheeses
moulds, mould-ripened cheeses 156, 182
mountain cheeses 261
mozzarella 22, 23, 114, 115
    The definitive margherita pizza 136
    Mozzarella in carozza 124
    Mozzarella di Bufala Campana DOC 23, 115
mushrooms, Linguine with mushrooms and stinky cheese 174

N
natural cheesemaking 142
Neuchâtel fondue 250
Not Ross's saag paneer 28

O
Oatcakes 272
onions
    Baked onions in brie custard 166
    Blue cheese and sweet onion pizza 198
    French onion soup with cheesy croutons 240
Ossau-Iraty AOC 22, 40, 205

P
paneer
    making 116
    Not Ross's saag paneer 28
Parish Hill Creamery, Vermont, USA 200–1
parmesan
    Stracciatella 242
    Two-cheese agnolotti with sage butter 248
Parmigiano Reggiano DOC 20–1, 53, 230, 258, 260
Passionfruit butter 68
pasta
    Linguine with mushrooms and stinky cheese 174
    Macaroni cheese 216
    Proper lasagne 258–60
    Two-cheese agnolotti with sage butter 248
'pasta filata' cheeses 114

pasteurisation 21, 132–4, 135
pastry
    Blue cheese, apple and leek pithivier 188
    Chorley cakes with cheddar cheese 262
    Egg, bacon and cheddar pies 214
    Fig, brie and rosemary tart 172
    Honey, whisky and saffron cheesecake 138
    Roast beetroot and feta tart 128
    Ross's ricotta shortcake 140
Pear, walnut and blue cheese salad with honey dressing 192
peas, Ricotta gnudi with buttery peas 126
pecorino 22, 40
    Brussels sprout slaw with pecorino 244
PDO and PGI cheeses 122
pies, Egg, bacon and cheddar pies 214
pizza
    Blue cheese and sweet onion pizza 198
    The definitive margherita pizza 136
    Pizza base 136
plums, Whey pops 144
polenta, Cheesy polenta with meatballs 168
Pont l'Évêque 159, 270
pork
    Cheesy polenta with meatballs 168
    Pork loin braised in milk 26
potatoes
    Aligot 212
    Tartiflette 170
Pouligny-Saint-Pierre 22, 158
Proper lasagne 258–60
Protected Appellations of Origin (PDO) 122
Protected Geographical Indication (PGI) 122
protein 21
puddings, Milk puddings with elderflower caramel 30

R
Raclette 168, 170
ragù 258
Ragusano 142, 218
raw milk 98
raw milk cheeses 98, 132
    arguments for and against 132–5
Reblochon AOC 170, 204
red wine, with cheese 270

rennet 110, 111
    coagulation 105–6
    types of 106
rice
    Arancini 120
    Yoghurt soup with chicken and rice 80
ricotta
    making 116
    Ricotta gnudi with buttery peas 126
    Ross's ricotta shortcake 140
    Two-cheese agnolotti with sage butter 248
Roast beetroot and feta tart 178
Roquefort 22, 182
Rye and molasses biscuits 268, 274

S
Sainte-Maure 158
Sainte-Maure de Touraine AOC 158
salads
    Blue cheese soufflés with pickled cherry and hazelnut salad 194
    Pear, walnut and blue cheese salad with honey dressing 192
Salers 142, 205, 218
Salt and pepper lavosh 276
salting (cheesemaking) 106, 109
sauces
    Béchamel 258, 260
    pizza sauce 136
    Simple lemon butter sauce for seafood 58
scones, Buttermilk scones 68
selecting and serving cheese 266–78
Selles-sur-Cher 158
semi-hard cheese recipes
    Aligot 212
    Best-ever cheese biscuits 222
    Cauliflower cheese 220
    Egg, bacon and cheddar pies 214
    Macaroni cheese 216
    Welsh rarebit 210
semi-hard cheeses 204–22
    benchmark 204–5
    making 206–8
Shankleesh 78
sheep breeds 38–40, 150
sheep's milk 22, 52, 142, 150
sheep's milk cheeses 22, 38, 40, 150–1, 182, 204, 205
Shish barak 82
shortbread, Butter shortbread 70

Shrikhand 94
Simple lemon butter sauce for seafood 58
skyr, Icelandic skyr, honey and cinnamon cake 96
snacks
    Blue cheese straws 186
    Cheese fricos 234
soufflés, Blue cheese soufflés with pickled cherry and hazelnut salad 194
soup
    French onion soup with cheesy croutons 240
    Stracciatella 242
    Yoghurt soup with chicken and rice 80
South American buttermilk doughnuts filled with dulce de leche 36–7
Spanish fried milk 34
sparkling wine, with cheese 270
starter cultures 105, 110
steak, Blue cheese steak sangers 190
Stichelton 183
Stilton 135, 182–3
stinky cheeses 158, 159
    Linguine with mushrooms and stinky cheese 174
storing cheese at home 267
Stracciatella 242
stretched curd cheeses 114
Sugar House Creamery, Upper Jay, New York 98–101
surface-ripened cheeses 156–74
    mould-ripened cheeses 156–8, 160–3, 165, 166, 172
    washed-rind cheeses 158–9, 168, 170, 174
sweet butter 53

T
Taleggio 159
Tartiflette 170
tarts
    Fig, brie and rosemary tart 172
    Roast beetroot and feta tart 128
    Ross's ricotta shortcake 140
temperature
    in cheese maturation 209
    keeping cheeses at home 267
terroir of cheese 135, 142
The Pines Dairy, Kiama, NSW 176–7
Tomme 204, 205, 212
Tongola Dairy, Cygnet, Tasmania 46–7

Two-cheese agnolotti with sage butter 248

U/V
unpasteurised milk 20
Valençay 22
vegetable rennet 106
vitamins 21

W
Wallaby kofta with cacik 86
washed-rind cheeses 158–9
    benchmark 159
    Cheesy polenta with meatballs 168
    Linguine with mushrooms and stinky cheese 174
    Tartiflette 170
Water crackers 278
Welsh rarebit 210
West Country Farmhouse Cheddar 204
Westcombe Dairy, Somerset, England 224–5
whey 21, 144
    Whey and soured cream bread 148
    Whey hot toddy 146
    Whey pops 144
whey butter 53
whey cheese 116
whisky
    Honey, whisky and saffron cheesecake 138
    Whey hot toddy 146
    with cheese 270
white-mould cheese, making 160–3
white wine, with cheese 270
wood and cheese 218
wrapping cheese 268

Y
yoghurt 74
    making 75
yoghurt recipes
    Bengali yoghurt fish curry 84
    Honey, lemon and cardamom frozen yoghurt 92
    Labneh 76
    Shish barak 82
    Shrikhand 94
    Wallaby kofta with cacik 86
    Yoghurt-marinated barbecue chicken 90
    Yoghurt soup with chicken and rice 80

287

Published in 2016 by Hardie Grant Books

Hardie Grant Books (Australia)
Ground Floor, Building 1
658 Church Street
Richmond, Victoria 3121
www.hardiegrant.com.au

Hardie Grant Books (UK)
5th & 6th Floors
52–54 Southwark Street
London SE1 1UN
www.hardiegrant.co.uk

A Cataloguing-in-Publication entry is available from the catalogue of the National Library
of Australia at www.nla.gov.au

Milk. Made.
ISBN 978 1 74379 135 6

Publishing Director: Jane Willson
Project Editor: Meelee Soorkia
Editor: Lucy Heaver, TUSK Studio
Design Manager: Mark Campbell
Designer: David Eldridge, Two Associates
In-house design: Andy Warren
Photographer: Alan Benson
Food Stylists: Michelle Crawford and Rhianne Contreras
Home Economist: Claire Pietersen
Production Manager: Todd Rechner

Colour reproduction by Splitting Image Colour Studio
Printed and bound in China by 1010